Contents

Acknowledgments

I am indebted to my good friend, The Rev. Morton T. Kelsey and my friend and colleague Gilda Frantz for reading the manuscript and giving me the benefit of their comments; and to my wife, Linny, for her many helpful suggestions, and to Helen Macey for her invaluable help with the preparation of this manuscript.

Introduction

The subject of men and women, of the nature of the masculine and the feminine, always arouses our interest, especially now, when men and women are trying, as never before, to understand themselves, and when the roles of the sexes and their relationship to each other are being reexamined. It is also a practical subject, promising to give us useful information that we can apply directly to ourselves and to our personal relationships.

One of the most important contributions of the Swiss psychiatrist C. G. Jung lies in this area. In his concepts of the anima and animus Jung makes a unique addition to our understanding of ourselves as men and women. In fact, it can be said that among the psychologists of this century only Jung has differentiated the psychology of men and women, and has shown us how they interrelate. It is because of the great interest today in the psychology of the sexes, and because there is no readily available volume that brings together Jung's most important ideas in this regard, that I have written this book.

It is for people to whom Jung's ideas on the masculine and feminine are new, as well as to those who already have experience in Jungian psychology and may be interested in the important discussions that have taken place regarding the masculine and feminine where the issues are not yet decided. Although I have tried to pull together the many threads of Jungian thought on this subject, the interested reader may wish to go more deeply

1

into it, so there is a selected bibliography at the back. Let this
book stand as an introduction, and a survey of a rich and varied
subject, but not as the final work in a field of knowledge that will
call for much more discussion and further investigation. In dealing with the masculine and the feminine we are, in the final analysis, discussing the human soul, and about this much more still
remains to be discovered.

Chapter One

Men are used to thinking of themselves only as men, and women think of themselves as women, but the psychological facts indicate that every human being is androgynous.[1] "Within every man there is the Reflection of a Woman, and within every woman there is the Reflection of a Man," writes the American Indian Hyemeyohsts Storm, who is stating not his own personal opinion, but an ancient American Indian belief.[2] The ancient alchemists agreed: "Our Adamic hermaphrodite, though he appears in masculine form, nevertheless carries about with him Eve, or his feminine part, hidden in his body."[3]

Mythology, and ancient traditions, which frequently express psychological truths that otherwise would elude our attention,

---

[1] The word *androgynous* comes from two Greek words, *andros* and *gynos,* meaning "man" and "woman" respectively, and refers to a person who combines within his or her personality both male and female elements. The word *hermaphrodite* is an analogous word. It comes from the Greek god Hermaphroditus, who was born of the union of Aphrodite and Hermes and embodied the sexual characteristics of both of them.

[2] Hyemeyohsts Storm, *Seven Arrows* (New York: Harper and Row, 1962), p. 14.

[3] From the alchemical treatise *Hermetis Trismegisti Tractatus vere Aureus,* 1610, quoted by C. G. Jung in *Letters, Vol. I, (Princeton, N.J.: Princeton University Press, 1973),* p. 443; and cf. *Letters, Vol. II, (Princeton, N.J.: Princeton University Press, 1975),* p. 321 n. 2.

4 *The Invisible Partners*

often state this belief in the sexual duality of human nature. In the Book of Genesis, for instance, we read that God was an androgynous being, and that the first human beings, being created in His⁴ image, were therefore likewise male and female: "On the day God created Adam," begins the fifth chapter of Genesis, "he made him in the likeness of God. Male and female he created them. He blessed them and gave them the name Man." We are also told in the second chapter of Genesis that when God wished to make woman He put Adam into a deep sleep, removed a rib from his body, and made Eve from Adam's rib. Clearly the original man, Adam, was thus both male and female. From this early division of the originally whole, bisexual human being comes the longing, through sexuality, for the reunion of the severed halves. The second chapter continues: "This is why a man leaves his father and mother and joins himself to his wife, and they become one body."⁵

This idea that the original human being was male and female is found in numerous traditions. For instance, both the Persian and Talmudic mythologies tell how God first made a two-sexed being—a male and a female joined together—and then later divided that being into two. This first, original man was often represented as having extraordinary qualities, as found in the extremely widespread image of the *Anthropos*, or Original Man, so often referred to in the writing of C. G. Jung and his colleagues.⁶ It is a thought expressed most succinctly, perhaps, in Plato's *Symposium*. Here Plato's character Aristophanes retells an ancient Greek myth about the original human beings, who were perfectly round, had four arms and four legs, and one head with two faces, looking opposite ways. These human spheres possessed such marvelous qualities and great intelligence that they rivaled the gods who, acting out of envy and fear, cut the spheres in two in order to reduce their power. The original, spherical beings fell

---

⁴ Wherever possible I will try to avoid using the *masculine* to refer to God or mankind, but common usage and the awkwardness of our language prevent my being completely consistent.

⁵ Gen. 2:24.

⁶ For a summary of the idea of the Anthropos see Marie-Louise von Franz, *Individuation in Fairy Tales* (Zurich: Spring Publications, 1977), pp. 90ff.

apart into two halves, one feminine and one masculine. Ever since then, so the story goes, the two severed parts of the original human being have been striving to reunite. "And when one of them meets his other half," Aristophanes informs us, "the actual half of himself, . . . the pair are lost in an amazement of love and friendship and intimacy, and one will not be out of the other's sight . . . even for a moment: these are the people who pass their whole lives together; yet they could not explain what they desire of one another."[7]

Storm's intuition that each man contains the reflection of a woman, and vice versa, is also reflected in shamanism. The shaman, the primitive healer or "medicine man," often has a tutelary spirit who assists him in the work of healing and teaches and instructs him in the healing arts. In the case of a male shaman, this tutelary spirit is female and acts like a spirit wife to him. In the case of a shamaness the tutelary spirit is male, and is her spirit husband, whom she has in addition to her flesh-and-blood husband. The shaman is unique partly because he or she has cultivated a special relationship to the other half of his or her personality, which has become a living entity, a real presence. A spirit wife says to her shaman husband, "I love you, I have no husband now, you will be my husband and I shall be a wife unto you. I shall give you assistant spirits. You are to heal with their aid, and I shall teach and help you myself." The shaman comments, "She has been coming to me ever since, and I sleep with her as with my own wife."[8]

Poets and philosophers, who often see things before the scientists do, also have intuited that a human being is androgynous. So the Russian philosopher Nicholas Berdyaev writes, "Man is not only a sexual but a bisexual being, combining the masculine and the feminine principle in himself in different proportions and often in fierce conflict. A man in whom the feminine principle was completely absent would be an abstract being, completely severed from the cosmic element. A woman in whom the mascu-

---

[7] *The Philosophy of Plato*, The Jowett translation, ed. Irwin Edman, *Symposium* (New York: The Modern Library, 1928), p. 356.

[8] Mircea Eliade, *Shamanism* (Princeton, N.J.: Princeton University Press, (1964), p. 72.

line principle was completely absent would not be a personality.
... It is only the union of these two principles that constitutes a
complete human being. Their union is realized in every man and
every woman within their bisexual, androgynous nature, and it
also takes place through the intercommunion between the two
natures, the masculine and the feminine."[9]

So this idea of man's androgynous nature is an old one that
has often been expressed in mythology and by the great intuitive
spirits of times past. In our century, C. G. Jung is the first scientist to observe this psychological fact of human nature, and to
take it into account in describing the whole human being.

Jung called the opposites in man and woman the *anima* and
the *animus*. By the anima he meant the feminine component in a
man's personality, and by the animus he designated the masculine component in a woman's personality. He derived these
words from the Latin word *animare*, which means to enliven, because he felt that the anima and the animus were like enlivening
souls or spirits to men and women.

Jung did not simply dream up his idea of the anima and
animus, nor did he allow his ideas to remain on the level of creative intuition, as did the Russian philosopher Berdyaev. Jung
was a scientist, and the scope of his scientific investigation was
the human psyche, hence his ideas are grounded on psychological
facts. Empirical evidence for the reality of the anima and animus
can be found wherever the psyche spontaneously expresses itself.
The anima and animus appear in dreams, fairy tales, myths, the
world's great literature, and, most important of all, in the varying
phenomena of human behavior. For the anima and animus are
the Invisible Partners in every human relationship, and in every
person's search for individual wholeness. Jung called them *archetypes*, because the anima and animus are essential building blocks
in the psychic structure of every man and woman. If something is
archetypal, it is typical. Archetypes form the basis for instinctive,
unlearned behavior patterns that are common to all mankind,
and represent themselves in human consciousness in certain typi-

---

[9] Nicholas Berdyaev, *The Destiny of Man* (New York: Harper Torchbooks,
1960), pp. 61–62.

cal ways. For Jung, the concepts of anima/animus explain a wide variety of psychic facts and form a hypothesis that is confirmed over and over again by empirical evidence.

Naturally, in any such discussion as this we come up against the question of what is meant by "masculine" and "feminine." Is there a difference between the masculine and feminine? Are the apparent differences between men and women due to archetypal, underlying psychological dissimilarities, or are they entirely the result of socially assigned roles and conditioning? In support of the latter idea it can be argued that the roles men and women play sometimes seem to be designated by the particular cultures in which they exist. It can be argued that men and women do what they do only because society assigns them that particular role or task. According to this point of view, there is no essential psychological difference between men and women, and it is only cultural influence that produces the apparent dissimilarities between the male and the female. In support of this contention is the fact that men can perform most of the functions women usually perform, except the biological functions associated with childbearing, of course, and women can also perform the way men do. The fact that women do not usually do what men do, and vice versa, is laid at the door of social expectation. In addition, there is the admitted difficulty of defining what is masculine and what is feminine, for as soon as a definition is offered there is always an objection, "But women (or men) sometimes act that way too."

The fact that men and women can perform many of the same functions in life supports the idea that each person is a combination of male and female polarities. Because of their feminine side, men can function in certain circumstances in ways traditionally regarded as feminine, and vice versa. This is a matter that will be considered in more detail later on.

On the other side of the discussion, the question of whether or not there is an archetype for the masculine and for the feminine—that is, whether essential psychological differences exist between the sexes and between the psychological polarities within each sex—is a matter to be decided by empirical evidence. Jung's view is that, while undoubtedly the cultural and social expectations and roles greatly influence the ways men and women live their lives, there are nevertheless underlying archetypal psychological patterns. The argument for this position will gradually unfold in the course of this book, and readers can decide the issue for themselves in terms of their own life experiences.

As for differentiating between what is the masculine and what is the feminine, it is perhaps best to talk in terms of images rather than in terms of psychological functioning. To speak of male and female is a way of saying that psychic energy, like all forms of energy, flows between two poles. Just as electricity flows between a positive and a negative pole, so psychic energy flows between two poles that have been called masculine and feminine. They are not always called masculine and feminine, however, and in this book the ancient Chinese terminology of *Yang* and *Yin* will sometimes be used instead. These terms are often more satisfactory because *Yang* and *Yin* are not defined in terms of role, or even in terms of psychological qualities, but by means of images. "Yang means 'banners waving in the sun,' that is, something 'shone upon' or bright." Yang is designated by heaven, the sky, the bright, the creative, the south side of the mountain (where the sun shines) and the north side of the river (which also receives the sunlight). On the other hand, "In its primary meaning Yin is 'the cloudy, the overcast.' " Yin is designated by the earth, the dark, the moist, the receptive, the north side of the mountain and the south side of the river.[10] Of course the Chinese also speak of Yang as the masculine and Yin as the feminine, but basically Yang and Yin represent the two spiritual poles along which all life flows. Yang and Yin exist in men and women, but they are also cosmic principles, and their interaction and relationship determine the course of events, as the Chinese wisdom book, the *I Ching*, clearly shows.

In a similar vein, the Chinese book of meditation, the *T'ai I Chin Hua Tsung Chih* [The secret of the golden flower], tells us of the two psychic poles in each man or woman. One is called the *p'o* soul and is represented by the kidneys, sexuality, and the trigram K'an (from the *I Ching*), and expresses itself as eros. The other, the *hun* soul, is represented by the heart, consciousness,

---

[10] *The I Ching or Book of Changes*, trans. Richard Wilhelm and Cary F. Baynes. (New York: Pantheon Books, 1950, 1966 ed.), p. xxxvi.

Boy, 9, is a big hit with Jackson routine

Michael Murphy, 9-year-old son of Larry and Mary Murphy, Urbana, will do his Michael Jackson impersonations in dance Saturday at the Clark County Fair.

His mother is the former Mary Freeman, who was a London resident. He also is the grandson of Mr. and Mrs. Allen Freeman of Danville rd, London, and the great-grandson of Mrs. Pauline McNeal, W. Center st, London.

Michael will perform at 8 p.m. at the Youth Building.

He also will give three performances on July 25—at 2:45 and 4:45 p.m. at the Youth Building and between 8 and 8:30 p.m. at the big tent.

Michael won a dance competition on WCOM-TV in Dayton Friday last week on the show "Easy Summer Nights." He will be on the show again Aug. 3 for finals competition.

Life Co. vs Harold E. Thomas, et al; order of confirmation and distribution; filed July 16.

Choctaw Lake Property Owners Association, Inc., vs Clifford Bruce, et al; entry correcting clerical mistake; filed July 16.

Chemical Mortgage Co. vs John H. Pannabecker Jr., et al; decree of foreclosure and order for sale; filed July 16.

COMMON PLEAS
Domestic Relations

Jerry Alan Flynn vs Keitha O. Flynn; defendant ordered to appear July 27, 8:30 a.m.; filed July 6.

Velma M. Carroll vs

Revised Code Sec. 2329.

The State of Ohio
Madison County

Thomas Hawkins, Plain vs. Rosemary Hawkins, fendant. No. 78DR-11-221.

In pursuance of an Or of Sale in the above enti action, I will offer for sal public auction, at the doo the courthouse in Lond Ohio, in the above nan County, on Friday, day of August, 1984, at 10 o'clock A.M., the follow described real estate, situ in the County of Madison a State of Ohio, and in Township of Union to-wit:

Beginning at a point in center line of State Ro 665, said point being and the fire trigram Li, and expresses itself as logos. These two poles fall away from each other if their energies are directed only outward, but if their energies are directed inward, through correct meditation, the two unite to form a higher and indestructible personality. In the translation of this Chinese text by the sinologist Richard Wilhelm, the two souls are also called anima and animus. Jung notes that the p'o soul is written with the characters for white and demon, and therefore it means "white ghost," and its principle belongs to the lower, earthbound nature so it is Yin. The hun soul is made from the characters for cloud and demon, and therefore it means "cloud-demon, a higher breath-soul," and so is Yang.[11]

We might wonder why, if men and women have always had a feminine and a masculine component, this fact has eluded the awareness of mankind in general for so many years. Part of the answer is that self-knowledge has never been one of our strong points. To the contrary, even the most elemental knowledge of oneself is something that most people resist with the greatest determination. Usually it is only when we are in a state of great pain or confusion, and only self-knowledge offers a way out, that we are willing to risk our cherished ideas of what we are like in a confrontation with the truth, and even then many people prefer to live a meaningless life rather than to go through the often disagreeable process of coming to know themselves. In addition, there are some aspects of ourselves that are harder to know than others. For instance, the shadow personality that is made up of unwanted and undeveloped characteristics, which could have become part of consciousness but were rejected, has long been recognized by the church. "The good that I would I do not, but the evil which I would not, that I do," cries out Saint Paul as he anguishes over his shadow.[12] It is not incredible to us that there is a darker side to our nature, because religion has so often pointed it out, though even here there is a remarkable conspiracy within most of us to pay lip service to our darker nature but avoid seeing

---

[11] See *The Secret of the Golden Flower*, trans. Richard Wilhelm, with a Foreword and Commentary by C. G. Jung, trans. from the German by Cary F. Baynes (New York: Harcourt, Brace and World, 1931, rev. ed. 1962), p. 115.

[12] Rom. 7:19 KJV.

it in the particular. So our shadow personality is often obvious to others, but unknown to us. Much greater is our ignorance of the masculine or feminine components within us that escape our attention because they are so entirely other than our consciousness. For this reason Jung once termed the integration of the shadow the "apprentice-piece" of becoming whole, and the integration of the anima or animus the "master-piece."[13]

But there also is another factor that makes knowledge of the anima or animus so elusive: These psychic factors within us are usually projected. Projection is a psychic mechanism that occurs whenever a vital aspect of our personality of which we are unaware is activated. When something is projected we see it outside of us, as though it belongs to someone else and has nothing to do with us. Projection is an unconscious mechanism. We do not decide to project something, it happens automatically. If we decided to project something it would be conscious to us and then, precisely because it is conscious to us, it could not be projected. Only unconscious contents are projected; once something has become conscious projection ceases.

So the anima and animus have, for the millennia of mankind's history, been projected onto mythological figures, onto the gods and goddesses who have peopled our spiritual world, and, perhaps most important of all, onto living men and women. The gods and goddesses of Greek mythology can be understood as personifications of different aspects of the masculine or the feminine archetype. Mythology has long been the way in which the human psyche personified itself, and as long as people believed in the living reality of their gods and goddesses they could, through appropriate ritual and worship, effect some sort of relationship to their psychic world.

When the anima and animus are projected onto other people our perception of them is remarkably altered. For the most part, man has projected the anima onto woman, and woman has projected the animus onto man. Woman has carried for man the living image of his own feminine soul or counterpart, and man has carried for woman the living image of her own spirit. This has led

---

[13] C. G. Jung, *Collected Works* [hereafter cited as *CW*] 9, 1, *The Archetypes and the Collective Unconscious* (New York: Pantheon Books, 1959), p.29.

to many unusual and often unfortunate consequences, since these living realities within ourselves often have a peculiarly powerful or irritating effect. So Jung said, in explaining part of the reason why the anima and animus have not been generally recognized as parts of the human personality, "In the Middle Ages, when a man discovered an anima, he got the thing arrested, and the judge had her burned as a witch. Or perhaps a woman discovered an animus, and that man was doomed to become a saint, or a savior, or a great medicine man. . . . Only now, through the analytic process, do the anima and animus, which were always outside before, begin to appear transformed into psychological functions."[14]

Because the anima and animus are projected, we do not usually recognize that they belong to us, for they *appear* to be outside of us. On the other hand, once the phenomenon of projection is recognized, these projected images can, to a certain extent, be taken back into ourselves, for we can use projections as mirrors in which we see the reflection of our own psychic contents. If we discover the anima or animus image has been projected onto a man or a woman, that makes it possible for us to see in reflection contents of our own psyche that otherwise might escape us. The capacity to recognize and utilize projections is especially important for self-knowledge when it comes to the anima or animus, since these psychic factors can never become so conscious to us that they do not project themselves. The contrasexual element within us is so psychologically elusive that it escapes our complete awareness, therefore it always is projected, at least in part. It cannot be a matter of knowing these realities so well that projection no longer occurs. This is an impossible goal, for the anima and animus do not partake of ego reality, but carry for us quite a different mode of psychological functioning. As far as self-knowledge is concerned, it is a matter of utilizing projections as mirrors, a task that is possible with the use of Jung's psychological concepts.

There is no one single place in which Jung wrote a definitive statement about the anima or animus. If you wish to find out what Jung had to say on the subject it is necessary to read many different passages in many different major works. Nor did Jung

---

[14] C. G. Jung, "The Interpretation of Visions," *Spring*, 1965, p. 110.

content himself with one single definition, but from time to time offered different ones. In doing so, however, he did not contradict himself, for each definition brings out a different aspect of these realities.

The simplest and earliest definition Jung offered is that the anima personifies the feminine element in a man, and the animus personifies the masculine element in a woman. He writes, "I have called this masculine element in woman the animus and the corresponding feminine element in man the anima."[15] Jung reiterated this early definition in *Man and His Symbols*, where he writes that "the anima is a personification of all feminine psychological tendencies in a man's psyche, such as vague feelings and moods."[16] He also speculates that the anima and the animus personify the minority of feminine or masculine genes within us. This thought occurs in several places in Jung's works. For instance, "The anima is an archetypal form, expressing the fact that a man has a minority of female genes, and that is something that does not disappear in him."[17] Of course the same thing could be said for the animus as a personification of the minority of masculine genes in a woman. That is, on the biological level, a man derives his masculine, physical qualities by virtue of having a slight plurality of masculine over feminine genes, and vice versa in the case of a woman. The anima, Jung has suggested, personifies on the psychological plane this minority of feminine genes, and, in the case of a woman, the animus personifies the minority of masculine genes.

If this is so, that which makes men and women different is not that men are entirely Yang and women Yin, for each sex contains the other within; it is the fact that a man ordinarily identifies his ego with his masculinity and his feminine side is uncon-

---

[15] C. G. Jung, *CW* 7, *Two Essays in Analytical Psychology* (New York: Pantheon Books, 1953), p. 88n.

[16] C. G. Jung, *Man and His Symbols* (Garden City N.Y.: Doubleday and Co., Inc., 1964), hardback ed. p. 177.

[17] *C. G. Jung Speaking*, ed. Wm. McGuire and R. F. C. Hull; (Princeton, N.J.: Princeton University Press, 1977), p. 296. Also cf.: *CW* 11, par. 48; *CW* 8, par. 782; CW 9, 1, p. 58 and p. 512.

scious to him, while a woman identifies herself consciously with her femininity, and her masculine side is unconscious to her.

The ego and the body carry, as it were, the same sign. A man's body is masculine, shaped by the male hormone and designed for certain functions; a woman's body is feminine, and is designed to perform certain specifically feminine functions, the most obvious being childbirth. The ego identifies with the masculine or feminine quality of the body, and so the other side, the anima or animus, becomes a function of the unconscious. This, at least, is the usual psychological development in men and women, though in some cases it may not be adequately achieved. A man may fail to develop a sufficiently masculine ego, for instance. In such a case, as we shall see, there may result a homogenized ego, a feminized masculinity, as it were, that may lead to a form of homosexuality.

All of this has important implications for the relationship between the sexes. As stated above, men, identified with their masculinity, typically project their feminine side onto women, and women, identified with their feminine nature, typically project their masculine side onto men. These projected psychic images are the Invisible Partners in every man-woman relationship, and greatly influence the relationship, for wherever projection occurs the person who carries the projected image is either greatly overvalued or greatly undervalued. In either case, the human reality of the individual who carries a projection for us is obscured by the projected image. This is especially the case with the anima and animus since these archetypes are so numinous. This means that they are charged with psychic energy, so that they tend to grip us emotionally. Consequently these projected images have a magnetic effect on us, and the person who carries a projection will tend to greatly attract or repel us, just as a magnet attracts or repels another metal. This leads to all kinds of complications in relationships, some of which will be examined in the last chapter.

Like all archetypes, the anima and animus have positive and negative aspects. That is, sometimes they appear to be highly desirable and attractive, and sometimes destructive and infuriating. In this they resemble the gods and goddesses who could shower mankind with gifts, but could also turn on mankind destructively. If the positive aspect of the anima image is projected by a man onto a woman, she then becomes highly desirable to him. She fascinates him, draws him to her, and seems to him to be the source of happiness and bliss. A woman who carries this projection for a man readily becomes the object of his erotic fantasies and sexual longings, and it seems to the man that if he could only be with her and make love to her he would be fulfilled. Such a state we call falling or being in love.

Naturally, a woman who carries such a powerful anima projection is pleased, at least at first. She feels flattered and valued, and, though she may be only dimly aware of it, enjoys a feeling of considerable power. The person who carries a projected psychic image from another person does have power over that person, for as long as a part of our psyche is perceived in someone else that other person has power over us.

The woman usually regrets the situation in time, however, as she experiences the disagreeable side of being the carrier of another person's soul. She eventually will discover that the man begins to suffocate her. She may find that he resents it when she is not immediately and always available to him, and this gives an oppressive quality to their relationship. She will also discover that the man resents any attempt on her part to develop her individual personality in such a way that it goes beyond the anima image he has placed on her, for, in fact, he sees her not as she actually is, but as he *wants* her to be. He wants her to fulfil and live out for him his projected feminine image, and this inevitably will collide with her human reality as a person. So she may find herself living in his box, fenced in by his determination that she fulfil his projection for him, and she may discover that the shadow side of his seeming love for her is a possessiveness and restrictiveness on his part that thwarts her own natural tendency to become an individual. When she insists on being herself she may find her man jealous, resentful, and pouting. She may also begin to dread his sexual advances, which, she begins to suspect, are not functions of the relationship between them, but have a compulsive, unrelated quality to them. Indeed, the two easily wind up at loggerheads regarding sex. The man is compulsively drawn to sexual relationship with the woman who carries his feminine image for him, and feels the relationship is complete only after coitus, when he feels a sense of momentary oneness with her. The woman, on the other hand, wants to work out the human relationship first and then give herself sexually to the man, and many devils whirl around this difference between them.

Moreover, the opposite projection can replace the positive one suddenly and without warning. The woman who at one time carried the projection of the positive anima, the soul image, for a man, may suddenly receive the projection of the negative anima, the image of the witch. All a man has to do is blame her for his own bad moods and suddenly he will see her in this light, and men, unfortunately, are notorious for putting the responsibility for their bad moods on women. Moods in a man, as will be seen, are disagreeable effects that descend on him from his feminine side. Being, as a rule, unenlightened about their own psychology, most men project the blame for these bad moods onto their women, which accounts for the fact that a woman whom a man was once in love with and regarded as a goddess can just as easily be seen by him as a witch. She is then undervalued as much as she was once overvalued.

The same projections are made by women onto men, of course. If a woman projects onto a man her positive animus image, the image of the savior, hero, and spiritual guide, she overvalues that man. She is fascinated by him, drawn to him, sees him as the ultimate man and ideal lover. She feels completed only through him, as though it were through him that she found her soul. Such projections are especially likely to be made onto men who have the power of the word. A man who uses words well, who has power with ideas and is effective in getting them across, is an ideal figure to carry such animus projections from a woman. When this happens he then becomes bigger-than-life to her, and she is quite content to be the loving moth fluttering around his flame. In this way she misses the creative flame within herself, having displaced it onto the man.

The man who receives such projections may often not be worth them. For instance, Adolph Hitler seems to have received the animus projection from the women of his time. He had an archetypal quality when he spoke, and a fascinating power with words. I once asked a Jewish woman friend of mine, who had

gotten out of Nazi Germany just in time, how it was that the
German women were so ready to send their sons to Hitler to be
destroyed in his war machine, and why it was that they did not
object. She answered that they were so fascinated by his words
they would have done anything he asked.

If a man carries the positive animus projection for a woman
he may feel flattered; it can be an inflating experience to carry
such projections. We are all too willing to identify ourselves with
the powerful images projected on us, and in this way escape from
the much more humble task of recognizing the genuine boundaries of our personalities. But the man, too, may soon become
aware of the disagreeable aspect of carrying such projections. He
begins to feel the sticky, clinging, unreal quality that has attached
itself to the relationship. As Irene de Castillejo put it, if a woman
looks to a man to be the keeper of her soul it "only makes him
impatiently declare that she is reading more into the relationship
than exists."[18]

Jung also comments on what it is like for a man to carry an
animus projection. "When somebody has an animus projection
upon me," he comments, "I feel as if I were a tomb with a corpse
inside, a peculiar dead weight; I am like one of those tombs Jesus
speaks of, with all sorts of vermin inside. And moreover decidedly a corpse myself, one doesn't feel one's own life. A real animus
projection is murderous, because one becomes the place where
the animus is buried; and he is buried exactly like the eggs of a
wasp in the body of a caterpillar, and when the young hatch out,
they begin to eat one from within, which is very obnoxious."[19]
Jung refers to the animus as being buried when it is projected because it is dead as far as its conscious development as a psychological function is concerned.

As mentioned, the negative projections are just around the
corner. The same man who once seemed fascinating and magnifi-
cent can just as readily be seen to be an infuriating, frustrating
person. The positive projection falls away when familiarity ex-

---

    [18] Irene de Castillejo, *Knowing Woman* (New York: G. P. Putnam's Sons,
1973), p. 174.
    [19] C. G. Jung, *The Visions Seminars, Part Two* (Zurich: Spring Publica-
tions, 1976), p. 493.

poses the relationship to a healthy dose of reality, and the negative projection is right there to take its place. The man who once was overvalued now is undervalued. Once seen as a hero, he now becomes a demon who seems to be responsible for all the woman's disappointments in love and feelings of being belittled.

If both a man and a woman project their positive images onto each other at the same time, we have that seemingly perfect state of relationship known as being in love, a state of mutual fascination. The two then declare that they are "in love with each other" and are firmly convinced that they have now found the ultimate relationship. Such relationships can be diagrammed as follows:

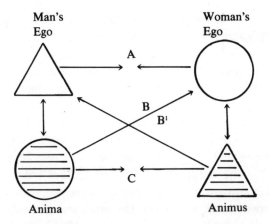

In this diagram it will be seen that there is a certain relationship on the conscious level between the ego personalities of the man and the woman, represented by line A. But there is also the powerful attraction between the two of them represented by lines B and B^1, which is the result of the projected images of the positive anima and animus. But the most powerful factor of all is line C, which is the attraction via the unconscious. Here it is as though the animus of the woman and the anima of the man have fallen in love with each other, and here is the bind, the powerful pull between them, the source of the magnetism of the being-in-love state.

There is much to be said for falling in love. Most of us can probably remember the first time we were in love, and what unexpected and powerful emotions were released. To have the experience of falling in love is to become open to matters of the heart in a wonderful way. It can be the prelude to a valuable expansion of personality and emotional life. It is also an important experience because it brings the sexes together and initiates relationship. Whether this leads to happy or unhappy consequences, life is kept moving in this way. Perhaps, especially with young people, falling in love is a natural and beautiful experience, and a life that has not known this experience is no doubt impoverished.

The fact is, however, that relationships founded exclusively on the being-in-love state can never last. As will be seen in chapter four, being in love is a matter for the gods, not for human beings, and when human beings try to claim the prerogative of the gods and live in a state of "in-loveness" (as differentiated from truly loving each other), there is a movement from the unconscious to break it up. A relationship of being in love simply does not last when put to the test of the reality of a true, human relationship; it can endure only in a fantasy world where the relationship is not tested in the everyday stress of real life. When they live together in everyday human conditions, "John and Mary" soon become real to each other as actual, imperfect human beings. The more real they are to each other as people, the less possible it is for the magical, fascinating images from the unconscious to remain projected on them. Soon the state of being in love fades away, and, worse yet, the same anima and animus who once fell in love with each other may now begin to quarrel.

The inability of the state of being in love to endure the stress of everyday human life is recognized by all great poets. This is why the relationship of Romeo and Juliet had to end in death. It would have been unthinkable for Shakespeare to have concluded his great love story by sending his loving couple to Sears to buy pans for their kitchen. They would have quarreled in an instant over what frying pan to choose and how much it was going to cost, and the whole beautiful love story would have evaporated. Great poets leave such love stories where they belong: in the hands of the gods. Or, if the human pair insists on living out the love fantasy, they may bring everything down around their heads in ruin. This is what Lancelot and Guinevere did in *Camelot*. Having fallen in love, they insisted on trying to make their love relationship a personal matter, to try to found their lives on it no matter what. As they tried to identify with and possess each other, and fulfil their love fantasies in a human sexual relationship, they brought down around them the ruin of Camelot. The great round table, depicting wholeness, was shattered, and the story of their love became the tragic story of the destruction of the beautiful castle and the downfall, not only of themselves, but of the noble King Arthur and many brave knights as well.

The fact that the state of being in love cannot endure the stress of everyday life is not what we want to hear, at least not in present-day America, which depicts the state of being in love as the goal of the relationship between the sexes, and constantly dangles it in front of our eyes with advertisements on television. Human beings are not very keen on substituting reality for the allurement of fantasies. We prefer to go on looking for the perfect man or woman, that is the man or woman who will fit our ideal image and guarantee that we are happy and fulfilled, even though it leads to disappointment after disappointment, and adds more and more bitterness to our cup of life.

It should now be clear that to the extent that a relationship is founded on projection, the element of human love is lacking. To be in love with someone we do not know as a person, but are attracted to because they reflect back to us the image of the god or goddess in our souls, is, in a sense, to be in love with oneself, not with the other person. In spite of the seeming beauty of the love fantasies we may have in this state of being in love we can, in fact, be in a thoroughly selfish state of mind. Real love begins only when one person comes to know another for who he or she really is as a human being, and begins to like and care for that human being.

No human being can match the gods and goddesses in all their shimmer and glory and, at first, seeing the person whom we love for who she or he is, rather than in terms of projections, may seem uninteresting and disappointing, for human beings are, on the whole, rather an ordinary lot. Because of this many people prefer to go from one person to another, always looking for the ultimate relationship, always leaving the relationship when the projections wear off and the in-loveness ends. It is obvious that with such shallow roots no real, permanent love can develop. To be capable of real love means becoming mature, with realistic expectations of the other person. It means accepting responsibility for our own happiness or unhappiness, and neither expecting the other person to make us happy nor blaming that person for our bad moods and frustrations. Naturally this makes real relationship a difficult matter, at which one must work, but fortunately the rewards are there too, for only in this way does our capacity for love mature.

This is not to say that projection is a bad thing. In itself, the projection of the anima and the animus is a perfectly natural event that will always occur. The anima and the animus are vitally alive in our psyches; as we have seen, they will never be so well known to us that they do not project themselves onto members of the opposite sex. In this way, via the projection, they become visible to us. Each time projection occurs there is another opportunity for us to know our inner, Invisible Partners, and that is a way of knowing our own souls. There is also the fact that, as has already been noted, projection is often the factor that first draws the sexes together. Man and woman are so unlike that it takes quite a power of attraction to bring them together in the first place; projection provides this influence because of the fascination with which it endows the member of the other sex. For this reason most love relationships begin with projection, and this serves life for then life moves. The question is, what happens then? Does that relationship become a vehicle for the development of consciousness, or do we give in to our infantile nature and go on and on through life insisting that somewhere there must be a relationship that offers us perfect bliss and fulfillment? Projection in itself is neither good nor bad; it is what we do with it that counts.

Two examples from history help us here. Dante and Mark Antony are both classic examples of men whose anima was projected onto women, but they dealt with their projections in very different ways. When he was only nine years old, according to Boccaccio, Dante met Beatrice (who was also nine). Instantly he fell in love with her. When we fall in love with someone instantly we can be sure a projection is involved, for how could we love someone whom we do not yet know? The following idealized description of her, which Dante wrote some years later, shows the powerful influence on Dante of the projected anima image:

> Her dress on that day was of a most noble color, a subdued and goodly crimson, girdled and adorned in such sort as suited with her very tender age. At that moment I say most truly that the spirit of life, which hath its dwelling in the secretest chamber of the heart, began to tremble so violently that the least pulses of my body shook therewith; and in trembling it said these words: *Ecce deus fortior me, qui veniens dominabitur mibi* (Behold a deity stronger than I, who, coming, will rule me) ... From that time forward Love quite governed my soul.[20]

It was not until Dante was eighteen that he again saw Beatrice. After the second meeting he wrote of her:

> ... it happened that the same wonderful lady appeared to me dressed all in pure white. And passing through a street, she turned her eyes thither where I stood sorely abashed; and by her unspeakable courtesy ... she saluted me with so virtuous a bearing that I seemed then and there to behold the very limits of blessedness. ... I parted thence as one intoxicated.

Then Dante adds significantly:

> Then, for that I had myself in some sort the art of discoursing with rhyme, I resolved on making a sonnet.[21]

This practically ended the relationship between Dante and Beatrice, if we can call such a cursory encounter a relationship, but it began Dante's relationship with his soul, and launched him on his astounding and vigorous career as a poet. Dante wrote many of his beautiful sonnets to Beatrice, and in his crowning work, *The Divine Comedy*, Beatrice reappears as his guide through heaven. The fact that at the age of twenty-three Beatrice

---

[20] Dante, *La vita nuova* [The new life], as quoted in *The Age of Faith* by Will Durant (New York: Simon and Schuster, 1950), p. 1059.
[21] Ibid.

married someone else and a year later died did not discourage him in the slightest. Dante had turned his encounter with the anima, which had fallen on Beatrice, into hard and creative work and it kept him going for a lifetime.

The experience of the Roman general Mark Antony was quite different. After the assassination of Julius Caesar in 44 B.C., Caesar's adopted son, Octavian, became emperor in the West and Antony in the East. Antony went to his new domain to receive the homage of the various kings and queens who were now subject to his rule, among whom was Cleopatra, the Queen of Egypt. Will Durant says of her, "Cleopatra was a Macedonian Greek by origin, and more probably blonde than brunette. She was not particularly beautiful; but the grace of her carriage, the vivacity of her body and her mind, the variety of her accomplishments, the suavity of her manners, the very melody of her voice, combined with her royal position to make her a heady wine even for a Roman general. She was acquainted with Greek history, literature, and philosophy; she spoke Greek, Egyptian, Syrian, and allegedly other languages, well; she added the intellectual fascination of an Aspasia to the seductive abandon of a completely uninhibited woman."[22] Cleopatra, who was supposed to be the conquered one, became the conqueror, as she sailed up the river Cydnus to meet Antony "in a barge with purple sails, gilded stern, and silver oars that beat time to the music of flutes and fifes and harps. Her maids, dressed as sea nymphs and graces, were the crew, while she herself, dressed as Venus, lay under a canopy of cloth of gold."[23] When Antony met this "seductive apparition" he fell in love with her at once, and thus began one of the most famous, and tragic, love affairs of history.

Cleopatra became as his soul to Antony, and as a consequence enjoyed enormous power over him. Antony was disastrously weakened because he could experience his soul only as it was projected onto Cleopatra, and from this time his qualities of generalship and leadership deteriorated. Until now, Antony had been a renowned military leader whose courage and dedication to

[22] Will Durant, *Caesar and Christ* (New York: Simon and Schuster, 1944), p. 187.

[23] Ibid., p. 204.

his army had won the fierce loyalty of his troops. However lamentable might have been Antony's wanton and pleasure-seeking ways in times of peace, in war the best in him came out and he proved himself a man of courage and an excellent general. Now Antony lost that quality of decisiveness which must mark the successful military man. For instance, when he had the Parthians at a marked disadvantage, and might have defeated them with a decisive campaign, he chose instead to postpone the struggle until his enemies had a chance to regroup their forces and resolve their internal disputes. He acted, according to Plutarch, "as a man who had no proper control over his faculties, who, under the effects of some drug or magic, was still looking back elsewhere."[24]

It was not long before Octavian and Antony had a falling out, and each marshaled his forces for a decisive battle. Antony had the superior army and was the more experienced general, while Octavian had built a new naval force and had won recent naval victories in the Western Mediterranean. Yet Antony chose to meet Octavian at sea because Cleopatra, who had a fleet of her own, wished it so. "So wholly was he now the mere appendage to the person of Cleopatra," writes Plutarch, "that, although he was much superior to the enemy in land-forces, yet, out of complaisance to his mistress, he wished the victory to be gained by sea."[25]

The two naval forces met at the famous battle of Actium in 31 B.C. Antony had parceled out his powerful army of over 100,000 men and placed them on board the great, unwieldly Oriental galleys that made up his fleet. Octavian met him with his fleet of smaller but much more maneuverable ships. Moreover, Antony's ships were manned by conscripts and inexperienced seamen, while Octavian's were manned by experienced and loyal Romans. Nevertheless, the battle might have been won by Antony had it not been for his excessive attachment to Cleopatra. Writes Plutarch, "But the fortune of the day was still undecided, and the battle equal, when on a sudden Cleopatra's sixty ships

---

[24] *Plutarch's Lives*, chapter on Mark Antony; The Harvard Classics edition, translated by Dryden, corrected and revised by Clough (New York: P.F. Collier & Son Company, 1909), p. 363.

[25] Ibid., p. 383.

were seen hoisting sail and making out to sea in full flight, right through the ships that were engaged. . . . The enemy was astonished to see them sailing off with a fair wind toward Peloponnesus. Here it was that Antony showed to all the world that he was no longer actuated by the thoughts and motives of a commander or a man, or indeed by his own judgment at all, and what was once said as a jest, that *the soul of a lover lives in someone else's body*, he proved to be a serious truth. For, as if he had been born part of her, and must move with her wheresoever she went, as soon as he saw her ship sailing away, he abandoned all that were fighting and spending their lives for him, and put himself aboard a galley of five ranks of oars, . . . to follow her that had so well begun his ruin and would hereafter accomplish it."[26]

Antony's forces, disheartened by the flight of their leader, lost the battle. For a time his remaining troops reassembled on land and held fast, waiting for their leader to return. But when Antony failed to come back to lead them, even his most loyal soldiers joined the side of the victorious Octavian. Meanwhile Antony, sunk in depression, had returned to Egypt, there to await his doom. Within a few months both Antony and Cleopatra were dead by their own hands.

The difference in outcome between the lives of Dante and Antony can be attributed to the ways in which they responded to the projection of the anima. Both men experienced the power of the anima as she projected herself onto a mortal woman. Dante, however, turned the experience into creative work, and realized his Beatrice as a figure of his own soul. Antony was unable to experience his soul except through projection, which led him into a life of pleasure and idleness, and so unmanned him that he lost the integrity of his personality.

These two examples are drawn from the annals of history, but the projection of the anima and the animus, and the resulting complications in the relationships of men and women, are also the daily fare of the psychotherapist. Eleanor (I shall call her), a woman in her mid-twenties, came for counseling because her husband had left her for another woman. A large but attractive woman, she had been married for about seven years. Her hus-

---

[26] Ibid., p. 387. Italics mine.

band had been away on a cruise with the navy when he wrote to her and said he was not coming back, but was going to the woman in another part of the country whom he "had always loved." For seven years, he now told his wife, he had done nothing but think of this other woman and now he was going to find her even though it meant giving up his relationship with his wife. He explained to Eleanor that though he liked her he did not "love" her, but was "in love" with the other woman. It made little difference to him that this other woman was already married and had several children.

He succeeded in finding his long-dreamt-of love and managed to persuade her to leave her husband and live with him. Perhaps she and her husband had a poor relationship, or maybe she was flattered to think that a man would love her for seven years and come gallantly across the country to marry her. Meanwhile, Eleanor had had enough. Although she deeply felt the rejection, she gained sufficient strength and self-confidence to decide that she could get along without her husband, especially if his relationship to her had such shallow roots. There were no children involved in her marriage, and she filed for a divorce. The relationship between Eleanor's husband and the woman he had "loved" for so long lasted all of eleven weeks. Then it was over, and he was writing Eleanor again explaining that he had been "disillusioned." Eleanor decided not to take him back.

Although I did not meet the husband, the story had all the hallmarks of a classic case of anima projection. The woman of whom the young man dreamt for seven years was not the actual flesh-and-blood woman he lived with for eleven weeks, but the elusive anima image in his mind. Unfortunately, he could experience his soul only through projection and, evidently, lacked the psychological depth and moral maturity to place real relationship above his fantasies and the longings inspired in him by his awakened anima. Had he been able to see his situation differently, he might have recognized that the anima, the image of his soul, was trying to reach him via his love fantasies for the distant woman, for it is through just such fantasies that the anima first seeks to become conscious to a man.

Another young woman came for counseling because of certain somatic complaints that were psychogenic in nature. Jane, as

I shall call her, had been divorced for about a year; she had one child. It seems that she had liked her husband perfectly well, but had fallen in love with another man. Apparently he also loved her and the two planned to divorce their spouses and marry each other. Jane divorced first and waited for her lover to join her, but time went by and he stalled. Finally he told her that while he did "love" her, he did not love her enough to come home to her every night. He eventually divorced his wife, but married another woman instead of Jane. This left Jane all alone and very depressed. Without a husband to support her, she had to take a job as a secretary, a job she disliked greatly. When I asked her what she would like to do instead she replied, almost guiltily, "You know, I really just want to be a wife and mother." This was sad, for that is exactly what she was not able to be now, for although she had one child she had no husband, and had to spend most of her days at work rather than making a home.

Jane reported several dreams in which the man with whom she had fallen in love came to her as a lover. She took these dreams literally, as personifications of the love relationship between the two of them. In doing this, she missed their inner, psychological meaning, for the man in the dream can be understood as her creative animus, a personification of her own creative powers that now want union with her. (In dreams, sexual union frequently represents the tendency of some part of us to unite itself to our conscious personality.) If Jane had understood these dreams properly she would have realized that had her creative powers been awakened, the projection of these creative powers onto the outer man could have been resolved, and her life would have taken a different direction. By choosing instead to live out her longings concretely, through the man who carried for her the projected image of the creative animus, she chose an unconscious path instead of a conscious one, and this almost always results in a disaster or, at least, in some kind of mischief. Because she missed the real point of her experience she failed to realize a certain potential in herself that was seeking actualization in her life. Fortunately she is young, and hopefully life will send along other opportunities.

What Jane experienced is very common. As Marie-Louise

von Franz points out,[27] when there is a certain creative energy in us that is spilling out over the edges or boundaries of the marriage and family life, it typically becomes projected onto a person of the opposite sex. This leads to the attraction to, and fascination with, that person, as has been discussed. When this occurs, one needs to examine closely what is happening. Am I married to the wrong person? Do I want to get away from my husband or wife and live permanently with the other person? Or, is the other person a hook onto whom my creative powers, which are not completely satisifed in the marriage, are projected? If the answer to the first two questions is affirmative, perhaps realistic changes need to be made in one's life. If the last question applies, the projection of the creative energies needs to be withdrawn so they can be fruitfully realized as a potential within oneself.

What happened to Jane can also be understood in terms of the disparity that almost always occurs in a relationship such as marriage. One person is more contained in such a relationship than the other, as C. G. Jung brought out in his article on marriage.[28] For the person who is contained in the relationship, emotional and physical needs are satisfied; there is no need to go beyond the relationship, for that person feels comfortably fulfilled. For the container, however, there is a tendency for libido to spill out over the boundaries of the relationship and seek an outlet elsewhere. This psychic energy that spills out is a creative energy that, as just noted, readily becomes projected onto another person unless it finds a suitable outlet. It is important that the container in such a relationship realize that the deepest longing is for unity of the personality, a unity that, as Jung has pointed out in his article, is available to the contained person via the relationship, but that the container must seek in another way.

Often the personality of the container is more complex and developed than that of the contained person. However, some-

---

[27] Marie-Louise von Franz, *The Feminine in Fairy Tales* (Zurich: Spring Publications, 1972), pp. 13ff.

[28] C. G. Jung, "Marriage as a Psychological Relationship," *CW* 17, *The Development of Personality* (New York: Pantheon Books, 1954), p. 189 of the 1964 edition.

times roles switch, and there are relationships in which now one person, now the other, is the container; or perhaps the wife is contained spiritually in the husband and the husband contained emotionally in the wife, or vice versa. Each person has a struggle. For the one who is contained there is anxiety and distress because that person senses, consciously or unconsciously, that the partner is not in the relationship as much as he is. For the person who is the container there is a sense of frustration, and sometimes feelings of guilt or disloyalty because of an awareness that he or she is not responding to the partner as the partner would like. Either the man or the woman may be the container for the other. It does not seem to be a matter of sex that determines which person plays which role, but rather a matter of which person has the more differentiated personality.

Naturally, if one person is the container, and the other the contained, this places a certain stress on the relationship and is part of a force that tends to draw people away from each other, rather than toward each other. In every relationship there are certain factors tending to promote the togetherness of the people, their oneness and desire to be together, and other factors tending to pull them apart. It is helpful to look at the latter factors as belonging to the principle of individuality, not as being entirely negative. A relationship is the joining together of two people. This is one side of life, but the other side of life calls for the accentuation of an individual personality, and for this to develop there must be the assertion and recognition of individual differences.

One rather frequent fantasy that married people find going through their minds is the fantasy that their partners are dead. The fantasy may consist in the simple thought, "What if my husband/wife should die?" Or it may develop into a fantasied scene of death, or even a wish that the other person would die. Naturally such fantasies shock us, and we tend to repress them quickly, horrified that we should have such a thought. But in most cases such fantasies are simply a compensation for a relationship in which the lives of the two people are too intertwined, and there is a need for more individual development. This same thought was expressed by Jesus in a statement that would be shocking unless we took it as a way of stating the importance of individual psychological development: "If any man comes to me without hating his father, mother, wife, children, brothers, sisters, yes and his own life too, he cannot be my disciple."[29]

The need for individual development does not invalidate relationship. Only separated beings can relate. Unless there is individual development on the part of two people, true relationship cannot occur. Instead, a state of mutual identification develops that blunts the psychological development of both partners. Nevertheless, when the principle of individuality asserts itself in a relationship it is important that the two people involved are able to discuss their differences and accept them. It also helps if the two people have certain things in common. A marriage, for instance, tends to hold together more often if the man and the woman share a common racial, religious, and educational background. Common goals also help, such as the goal of raising children, or a commonly shared financial goal. Having friends in common is also helpful.

Every relationship is a mixture of areas where people meet and areas where they do not meet because the two people are different. Verda Heisler, author of the helpful article "Individuation through Marriage,"[30] diagrams the situation in this way:

A

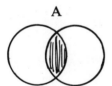

B

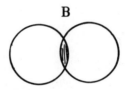

In this diagram, the areas that are shaded represent areas in which the man and woman share interests, goals, or aspirations in common. The white sections represent areas where there are individual differences. The amount of overlap may be greater or less. So diagram *A* shows a relationship in which there is more psychological life shared in common than in diagram *B*.

Clearly these Invisible Partners have a fateful effect on relationships. As we have seen, when they are projected the anima

---

[29] Lk. 14:26.

[30] Verda Heisler, "Individuation through Marriage," *Psychological Perspectives*, Fall 1970, Vol. 1, No. 2.

and animus can produce extraordinary attractions and repul-
sions between men and women, and invariably mislead a man or
woman into thinking too much or too little of his or her partner.
But the anima and animus also produce their marked effects
on the consciousness of men and women quite apart from projection, and here too they have disturbing effects on relationships. It
is to this that I now turn.

Chapter Two

Myths and fairy tales, being spontaneous representations of psychological reality, often represent the anima and animus, and through their vivid story imagery show us how they can affect human life. Take, for instance, the Greek myth of Circe, who was a deadly female being, known for her enchantments and evil spells. She had poisoned her husband and gone to live in a beautiful castle on the isle of Aeaea. By means of magic, she had the power to enchant any man who wandered onto the shores of her island, and she could turn him into an animal. The most famous story about Circe is found in the *Odyssey*. Odysseus's men have ventured onto the isle and have been welcomed by Circe, who entertains them and gives them a glorious banquet in her palace, but just at the height of their pleasure and enjoyment Circe casts her evil spell on the men and they are turned into swine. Odysseus himself, fortunately, had been forewarned by the god Hermes, who provided him with an herb that was an antidote to the spells of Circe. Thus prepared, Odysseus is finally able to get the better of Circe and compels her to free his men from her evil spell. But even then her fascination is so great that Odysseus dallies with her on the island for a year, forgetting about his wife, Penelope, and the urgency of his voyage back to his homeland.

The Sirens, whom we also meet in the *Odyssey*, were as dangerous as Circe. The Sirens were fearsome female creatures with bodies of birds and heads of women. They could make exceeding-

ly melodious music, which was so enticing that no man who
heard their music could resist going to them. But once a man ap-
proached them the Sirens set upon him and tore him apart, add-
ing his bones to the heap of skeletons that were scattered over
their terrible island. Odysseus himself would have fallen prey to
the Sirens had he not been forewarned by Circe. When his ship
passed the island where the Sirens lived he had his men stop up
their ears so they could not hear the deadly music, while he himself was lashed securely to the mast. In this way, though he heard
the music, he was able to pass safely by.

In both of these tales we have female beings who are extremely dangerous to men. They have great seductive power, and
can lure men with their offerings of pleasure or music into a state
of unconsciousness. Then, once the men are seduced and powerless, they destroy them. The transformation of Odysseus's men
into swine represents the reduction of masculine consciousness to
its lowest, most swinelike nature, and a psychological state in
which a man has become identical with his appetite for sex and
pleasure. The rending apart of men by the Sirens personifies the
way the deadly anima power can tear masculine consciousness
into shreds by luring men into a state of unconsciousness with offerings of bliss and pleasure. In this way Greek mythology personified the deadly, dangerous side of the anima that can lure a
man to his destruction. We could say that Mark Antony fell prey
to the evil effects of the anima in her Circe and Siren aspect, for
he became identical with his appetites for pleasure, and was lured
to his destruction by the sirenlike quality of the anima he projected onto Cleopatra.

Odysseus is able to escape this evil fate because he has been
forewarned, that is, he has become conscious of the meaning of
the situation. Equipped with his knowledge of the deadly nature
of Circe, the hero is able to overcome her dangerous side and experience her helpful side, since it is she who warns him about the
Sirens and tells him how to find safe passage. Odysseus's men,
who represent ordinary consciousness, do not hear the Sirens'
music, but Odysseus does. The hero is the man who is fully ex-
posed to the anima and her effects, but is psychologically enlight-
ened and so does not fall prey to her negative side.

A striking example of the dangerous side of the animus is in the story of Tobit, which is found in the *Apocrypha*. The story tells us of the beautiful young woman, Sarah, who is possessed by a demon, Asmodeus. Seven times Sarah had been married, but each time the demon Asmodeus had come on her wedding night and strangled her husband. Sarah prays to God, who hears her prayer and resolves to help her. He also hears the prayer of the righteous, blind old man, Tobit, and his son, Tobias, and sends the angel Raphael to help the old man and his son, and the young woman Sarah.

Raphael takes Tobias on a journey and on the way they come to a river. Tobias goes down to the river to wash and as he does so a fish leaps up and would have swallowed him had not Raphael cried out, "Catch the fish."[1] Tobias catches the fish and throws it onto the land and, acting on the instructions of the angel, cuts out the heart, liver, and gall, and takes them with him. Eventually they arrive at Sarah's home where Tobias is told by Raphael that he is to marry the young woman. At first Tobias objects. "I have heard," he complains, "that the girl has been given to seven husbands and that each died in the bridal chamber. . . . I am afraid that if I go in I will die as those before me did, for a demon is in love with her, and he harms no one except those who approach her."[2] But the angel instructs him to take the heart and liver of the fish and make a smoke of them, and tells him that when the demon smells the smoke he will flee to the remotest parts of the earth. Tobias does as he is told. He falls in love with Sarah, marries her, and that evening makes a smoke of the heart and liver of the fish, and Asmodeus, smelling it, is banished.[3]

Asmodeus personifies the animus, who, when he is in possession of a woman, acts like a demon. We are likely to be possessed by an unconscious content when we are ignorant of it and have no relationship to it, but it helps us when we are related to it. Becoming conscious or aware of the contents of the unconscious is the surest way to establish a relationship. It has been

---

[1] Tobit 6:3, RSV.

[2] Ibid., 6:13–14.

[3] The gall of the fish is used later in the story to cure the old man, Tobit, of blindness.

said of the complexes that make up the unconscious that most people wonder if they have any complexes; what they do not know is that their complexes have them. So Asmodeus *has* Sarah and it is because he possesses her that he is a demon. He destroys her seven husbands because the animus, when he possesses a woman, is destructive to human relationships and to eros values.

The angel and the fish symbolize the healing powers of the unconscious, and, more specifically, the power of a spiritual life. As Jung once pointed out, one antidote to possession by evil is to have one's soul filled with a spirit more powerful than that of evil. When Tobias heats the gall and liver of the fish and sends up a smoke, it is as though a new spiritual force enters into Sarah's soul, and there is now no room for the evil, demonic force. Tobias, of course, also arouses Sarah's eros, and brings up her feeling for a man and for relationship. This human warmth and eros also have the capacity to banish the evil power. So the story gives us a clue about how a woman can destroy the deadly effects of the animus: Her soul must be filled with a more powerful spirit than that of the destructive animus, and her capacity for eros and relationship must live.

The demon Asmodeus, the sorceress Circe, and the seductive Sirens symbolize the destructive effects of the animus and anima. It is usually these negative effects that we first experience and that must be overcome if the positive aspects of the Invisible Partners are to be realized. The negative, destructive effects constitute the "bad news" about the animus and anima, so they will be considered first and the "good news," the helpful, positive side of the anima and animus, reserved for the next chapter.

The negative effects of the anima and animus are directly related to a man's unawareness and devaluation of his feminine side, and a woman's unawareness of her masculine side. With men, the anima tends to take them over in proportion to their failure to properly recognize and respect feminine values in themselves, in life, and in women. For this reason, men need to learn to talk with women and to listen to them, for a woman can then instruct a man in what is important to her; in this way he becomes more related to eros and its values. This facilitates his proper relationship to the anima, an important matter, for in dealing with archetypal figures of the unconscious the key is relatedness. For, as we have seen, when such figures are related to consciousness their positive side tends to be manifested, otherwise their demonic side tends to appear.

In the case of the anima, it is she who lies behind a man's moods. When a man is possessed by the anima he is drawn into a dark mood, and tends to become sulky, overly sensitive, and withdrawn. A poisonous atmosphere surrounds him, and it is as though he is immersed in a kind of psychological fog. He ceases to be objective or related, and his masculine stance is eroded by peevishness. If a man argues or writes in this frame of mind, this peevishness and poison will certainly emerge. In writing, the influence of the anima can be seen in sarcasms, innuendos, irrelevancies, and poisonous jabs that reveal a subjective, personalistic bias and detract from the objective quality of the work. A man in the grip of the anima acts for all the world like an inferior kind of woman who is upset about something and that, in fact, is exactly what he has within himself.

Such a mood may fall on a man in an instant. A seemingly chance remark from someone, a slight, an almost unnoticed disappointment, and suddenly a man may be in a mood. Astonishingly enough, men almost invariably fail to note that something from within themselves has suddenly possessed them, that a mood has fallen on them and gripped them, and that the event has been quite autonomous. Such moods may simply make the man a bit grouchy or out of sorts for a while, or they may become dangerously dark. If the moods are chronic they may lead a man into alcoholism or severe depression. Under certain circumstances, an intense anima mood may plunge a man into such a feeling of hopelessness that he commits suicide. It is no doubt the presence of the anima within a man that explains why fewer men than women attempt suicide, but more men than women actually succeed in killing themselves. It is as though the anima says, "It is all futile!" and the man falls into utter despair.

The woman in a man's life could tell him a lot about these anima moods. She knows almost right away when a mood has her man because then he is not available for relationship. One cannot get through the mood to find the man. It is as though he has disappeared, and someone else has taken his place. This moodiness of the man has, as a result, a disturbing effect on a woman, who finds it diffucult to be with a man who is in such a state.

If you can get to the bottom of a man's mood you will find that something has gone wrong, but the man may hardly realize what it is. It may be that his inner woman does not like what the man is doing. For instance she may not like his work because it drains her of life and energy, or it may keep her from her fulfillment in life. It is as though the man's inner woman, and the woman's inner man, also need to be fulfilled in life, but the only way they can be fulfilled is through the kind of life their outer man or outer woman leads. Imagine a woman who is denied her proper scope in life, who is forced to endure a way of life that leaves her no room for her emotions or her own creative powers. Such a woman would, naturally, become dissatisfied and her displeasure would be felt in the bad atmosphere she would create. It is exactly this way with the anima if she does not have enough share in the man's life.

But the negative anima mood may also be a function of a relationship. For example, a man may get thrown into this mood when his feelings have been hurt. Someone has ignored him, given him a nasty verbal thrust, or rejected him in some way, and he is hurt and angry. When the man is hurt, if he were to express his feelings directly he would be all right—he would not go into a mood. If it is his wife who has hurt his feelings, for instance, and if he were to say to her, "That really made me angry when you said that," he would be himself and would not become possessed by the anima; he would not fall into a mood about it. But if the man does not express his feelings, they fall into the unconscious, and the anima gets them. The anger that the man did not express directly is taken over by the anima, who turns it into resentment; in fact, resentment in a man is always a sign of the anima at work. In the hands of the anima this unexpressed and unresolved anger smolders, burns, and eats away at him, and is expressed indirectly by "passive-aggressive" moods and behavior. It is always ready to erupt into flames; then the man does not have his anger, it has him. He is possessed by rage, and his anger is in constant danger of becoming a terrible affect, for it is as though the anima stands poised to drop her flaming match into the waiting can of gasoline, and the man will erupt in an engulfing and uncontrolled emotion.

Jung noted that the anima can be seen to be at work wherever emotions and affects are at work in a man. He wrote, "She intensifies, exaggerates, falsifies, and mythologizes all emotional relationships with his work and with other people of both sexes."[4] The antidote for this, as has been mentioned, is for the man to know what he is feeling and become capable of expressing this in relationship. This keeps his emotion out of the clutches of the anima, and, moreover, satisfies her that the correct thing is being done with whatever it is that has wounded or aroused him. The anima does not necessarily want to carry the man's emotional life for him; she gets it by default. It is as though she says, "Why don't you say something about that irritating thing that so-and-so has just done to you! If *you* don't do something about it, *I* will." We can say that if something has gone wrong in an emotionally significant relationship the anima will grouse about it until the man straightens it out, or comes to terms with his emotions in some proper way.

Unfortunately, many men have difficulty expressing their feelings. Men tend to like their relationships to be smooth, easy, and comfortable. They are reluctant to get into emotionally toned discussions or difficult issues. They want "peace and quiet" and want their women to maintain a pleasant atmosphere and not bring up distressing matters. But, as we have just seen, if matters of relationship are ignored they simply get worse, and when a man consistently denies his feelings, and fails to relate them to the people in his life, he becomes a chronically moody, resentful, anima-ridden man. Then it is as though a witch has gotten him, for he has become identical with his moods.

If a man becomes capable of expressing his feelings, not only does he keep emotional matters out of the clutches of the anima, he also becomes a much more developed person. A man who al-

---

[4] Jung, *CW* 9, 1, p. 70.

ways avoids emotionally toned encounters with other people is contained within the Mother. One way for him to get out of his Mother complex is to express himself in relationship. If he fails to do so he remains emotionally a little boy who is afraid of women, who resents them if they don't keep him happy, and who is out of touch with his own masculine strength.

Men are often reluctant to bring up unpleasant things that have happened in a relationship with a woman because they are afraid of her anger, or their own anger, or they are afraid they will be rejected, or they are afraid of pain.

Working things out in relationship requires that a man must come to terms with his anger. He must become comfortable enough with anger so that he can express it without being overcome by it; he must be able to allow himself to have his own creative dark side. One man I know said that whenever a difficulty arose with his wife he positioned himself near the door so that when he became angry he could simply leave. He was that afraid of his own anger. Of course, until he could work this through with himself he would not be capable of working out his relationship with his wife.

If a man is afraid of his woman's anger it often goes back to the little boy in him. Watch a small boy when mother becomes angry at him! See how unpleasant it is for him, and how many little boys will be terribly hurt, and want to do whatever they can to appease mother so things will be good again, or, if they are more robust, will spew out boyish defiance so as not to be overwhelmed by their own hurt feelings. A woman's acid anger and power of rejection have enormous influence on other people, men and boys especially, and if a man is to become capable of relationship with a woman he must overcome his fear of her anger and his anxiety about being rejected. This may mean that he will have to find and help the little boy in himself. By recognizing his hurt-little-boy side he is much less likely to become identical with it, and can remain more the man in relationship with the woman in his life.

He will also have to deal with the angry, rejecting side of his woman. Why does she have to be that way? he may ask himself. But just as the anima has a negative side that must be overcome if the positive side is to be realized, so every man must be capable of enduring the dark side of the woman in his life if he is going to find her tender and life-giving side.[5]

A man's fear that he will be rejected if he brings up difficult matters in the relationship is usually unfounded. A woman who cares about a man, or is at all connected to her own instincts for relatedness, has a great capacity for confrontation and working things out. A young man who was working in a restaurant once had an angry encounter with one of the waitresses in which he told her just what he thought of her and some things she was doing. Afterwards he came to me in amazement and said, "You know, you can tell a woman anything you want as long as it is related." He was astonished that this girl had listened to what he had said, had responded to it, and had not just become angry at him or walked out on him.

Related anger means that the issues that are brought up are concerned with what is going on between two people. It is an honest expression of genuine feeling. If a man expresses anger in an unrelated way to a woman, he will do it indirectly by creating a bad atmosphere or indulging in a personalistic attitude. If he expresses anger in a *related* way, he will tell her just what it is that is upsetting him. If a woman cares about a man she will not reject him if he expresses his anger at her in this way; to the contrary, she will welcome it, for it shows that their relationship is meaningful to him. From a woman's point of view, if a man ignores matters of relationship it is the same as ignoring her, and that means to her that she and the relationship are not important to him.

Many times women will also welcome a man's anger because it tells them when they have gone too far. Where there is emotion, something is happening, and it means the other person is taking part in the relationship. When a man never shows any emotion he leaves a vacuum in the relationship, and, especially if

---

[5] By the way, every woman who is angry is not "in the animus" or animus-possessed. There is a tendency among men to suppose that all anger in a woman comes from the animus. This can operate as a subtle way to keep a woman from expressing those angry feelings that men dislike to face. As we will see, the animus may very well take up the cause of a woman's anger and express it for her, but the feminine is quite capable of being angry on its own.

he becomes passive, there is something in most women that will dominate such a man if he allows it. It is man's passivity in relationship that draws out a woman's animus. A man's anger may be his healthy reaction against domination, and this kind of anger a woman will be glad to receive, for in it she will recognize and respect her man's strength, and be liberated from her own instinctive tendency to dominate him. It is as though she says, "So that's the way it is. Now I can stop dominating him for he has become himself."

I have stressed here the way a woman appreciates a man's emotional reactions, but it can be the other way around, of course; it can be the man who yearns for a genuine emotional response from his woman. More often than not, it is the man who retreats emotionally from relationship, but this is a generalization with many exceptions.

On the other hand, if the anima gets hold of a man's emotions, as Jung said, she intensifies, falsifies, and exaggerates the whole matter. These distortions the anima creates in a man's mind have led James Hillman to challenge an oft-stated thesis among Jungian psychologists that men relate through the anima, that a man who has a "well-developed anima" will, as it were, relate through her to other people. Hillman contends that if we want relationship the anima should not be a part of it. "It seems odd," he writes, "that anima could ever have been considered as a help in human relationship. In each of her classical shapes she is a non-human or half-human creature and her effects lead us away from the individually human situation. She makes moods, distortions, illusions, which serve human relatedness only where the persons concerned shared the same mood or fantasy. If we want 'to relate,' then anima begone!"[6] It is the man himself who relates, and if the relationship is determined by the anima, it becomes a matter of archetypal fantasy playing itself out through human actors, or of the exaggerations and falsifications of emotions and emotionally toned issues that Jung has described.

The important thing to remember, as will be seen more clearly later on, is that the correct position of the anima is in-

---

[6] James Hillman, "Anima," *Spring,* 1973, p. 111.

ward, not outward. She belongs as a function of relationship between a man's consciousness and the unconscious, not as a function of relationship between a man and other people. When she intrudes into this outer sphere, there are difficulties. Men are quite capable of doing their own relating and having their own feelings, and do not need the anima to provide this for them.

The anima not only interferes with a man's emotional reactions, she can interfere with his thinking as well. For instance, when a man is anima-possessed he may begin to give forth *opinions* instead of genuine thinking. It is as though the anima begins to talk right through him, and she expresses herself as though she had an animus, which means that she expresses opinions without regard to facts, relationship, or logic. When a man is in this state of mind he begins to argue in a peevish way, and his masculine objectivity is quite lost in a sea of emotionally toned and irrational opinions that prove resistant to reasonable discussion. Jung pointed out that "men can argue in a very womanish way . . . when they are anima-possessed and have thus been transformed into the animus of their own anima."[7]

She may also disturb his thinking by infiltrating it with her own notions of what is desirable. The result is a kind of anima-thinking in which a man's capacity for clear distinctions is blurred, and his logos is distorted. It is as though the anima, in an effort to promote a kind of "togetherness," blurs over all distinctions and ignores all genuine differences. Then the man is not so much the victim of a mood as he is the victim of a powerful figure within himself that seeks to mould his conscious thinking and produces fuzziness instead of clarity, fog instead of vision.

Among the negative attributes of the anima is her capacity to poison a man's creative urges. When a man gets a creative idea or impulse that would lead him beyond the ordinary, a subtle voice seems to whisper in his ear a destructive thought that may well stop him in his tracks. Let us say that the man conceives an idea to write, and sees himself compiling a book or article. The anima is almost certain to whisper, "Who are you to think you can write?" Or, "But it has already been written." Or, "But no

---

[7] C. G. Jung, *CW* 9, 2, *Aion* (New York: Pantheon Books, 1959), p. 15.

one would ever publish it." The creative energy of many men is stolen from them by this subtle voice that seemingly wants to nullify a man's attempts to make something of himself.

Jung relates in his autobiography, *Memories, Dreams, Reflections,* that he heard such a poisonous voice speak to him when he was first beginning to work out a relationship with his unconscious personality through the use of the technique of active imagination.[8]

> When I was writing down these fantasies, I once asked myself, "What am I really doing? Certainly this has nothing to do with science. But then what is it?" Whereupon a voice within me said, "It is art." I was astonished. It had never entered my head that what I was writing had any connection with art.... I knew for a certainty that the voice had come from a woman. I recognized it as the voice of a patient, a talented psychopath who had a strong transference to me. She had become a living figure in my mind.
>
> Obviously what I was doing wasn't science. What then could it be but art? It was as though these were the only alternatives in the world. That is the way a woman's mind works.
>
> I said very emphatically to this voice that my fantasies had nothing to do with art, and I felt a great inner resistance. No voice came through, however, and I kept on writing. Then came the next assault, and again the same assertion: "That is art." This time I caught her and said, "No, it is not art! On the contrary, it is nature," and prepared myself for an argument....
>
> I was greatly intrigued by the fact that a woman should interfere with me from within.... Why was it thought of as feminine? Later I came to see that this inner feminine figure plays a typical, or archetypal, role in the unconscious of a man, and I called her the "anima."...
>
> At first it was the negative aspect of the anima that most impressed me. I felt a little awed by her. It was like the feeling of an invisible presence in the room.... What the anima said seemed to me full of a deep cunning. If I had taken these fantasies of the unconscious as art, they would have carried no more conviction than visual perceptions, as if I were watching a movie. I would have felt no moral obligation toward them. The anima might then have eas-

---

[8] See the Appendix at the back of this book for a description of active imagination.

ily seduced me into believing that I was a misunderstood artist, and that my so-called artistic nature gave me the right to neglect reality. If I had followed her voice, she would in all probability have said to me one day, "Do you imagine the nonsense you're engaged in is really art? Not a bit." Thus the insinuations of the anima, the mouthpiece of the unconscious, can utterly destroy a man.[9]

This engaging story from Jung not only illustrates how the anima can poison a man's consciousness and rob him of himself should he fall for her insinuations, it also gives us a hint about how a man can prevent the negative anima from having this destructive influence on him: by making her conscious. Later we will look more closely at what this means, and how a man can relate positively to the anima, and a woman to the animus. Meanwhile it can be seen that the negative anima is very much like a witch who can seduce a man into unconsciousness, and can turn him into stone by paralyzing his creative efforts.

If the anima is the master of moods in a man, the animus is the master of opinions in a woman. He typically expresses himself in judgments, generalizations, critical statements, and apodictic assertions that do not come from a woman's own process of thinking and feeling, but have been picked up from various authoritative sources, mother or father, books or articles, church or some other collective organization. It is the animus who is behind the autonomous, critical, and opinionated thoughts that intrude into a woman's consciousness. He thus represents inferior masculine logic, just as the anima represents inferior feminine emotionality.

In dreams the negative animus often appears as a group of men rather than as a single individual. Imagine a number of uneducated and uninformed men sitting around the cracker barrel expressing their opinions on politics or religion! This is the way the animus can sound. If a woman becomes identified with such opinions in herself, which happens when the animus is not differentiated from her own ego psychology, we speak of animus possession.

---

[9] C. G. Jung, *Memories, Dreams, Reflections* (New York: Pantheon Books, 1961), pp. 185–187.

The opinions of the animus have an unpleasant and even destructive quality, and may be projected onto other people, or directed inwardly on the woman herself. In the former case, other people cannot stand the woman because of the blunt and critical judgments she passes on them. In the latter case, the woman cannot stand herself, for the effect of the judgments of the animus on her is to destroy her sense of her own value and worth.

The animus is thus able to rob a woman of her creativity, even as the anima, as we have seen, can rob a man of his. At the moment when a woman gets a creative idea, or her eros and tenderness begin to stir in her in a new way, the animus may intrude into her consciousness with thoughts that could prevent her from fulfilling herself. He may say, "You can't do that." Or, "Other people can do these things much better than you." Or, "You have nothing of value to offer." If the woman identifies with such thoughts, that is, mistakes them for her own thoughts and for the truth, the new creative possibility is taken away from her.

It can be seen that the negative anima and animus seem to personify a destructive, negating force. Mythology has long pictured just such a psychological situation. For instance, in ancient Babylonia it was believed that when a soul was born into the world the gods appointed two gods and two goddesses to accompany that soul through life. The task of one god and goddess was to help and guide the soul. The task of the others was to try to negate and destroy the soul. In Judaeo-Christian lore this adversary or accuser who tries to destroy us is personified as Satan. In fact, the Greek word for the devil means "an accuser," or an "adversary." This is an accurate psychological portrayal of the way things are. There seems to be a power of evil within us that tries to negate and destroy us, and the negative anima and animus, the witch or sorcerer within us, seem to be a part of that force.

The opinions of the animus have a peculiarly irritating effect on other people because, in spite of their seeming logic, they do not fit the actual situation. Yet neither can they be reasoned with, for the animus has an absolutist attitude, and his opinions are not amenable to discussion or qualification. Whenever the animus takes over, a woman is taken away from her own thinking and feeling, and she becomes identical with banal statements, sweeping judgments, or generalizations. Small wonder, when these judgmental opinions are directed from within against herself, that a woman tends to become depressed and is robbed of the colorfulness of life.

A conversation in which the animus is involved might go like this: A man who is discouraged over some difficulty might express his sense of defeat and despair, and the woman might respond with, "Everyone tends to get discouraged now and then." This seemingly harmless statement, true enough in itself, will have the tendency to stop the man dead in his tracks. He will feel put off and not able to go on to express himself, and may feel vaguely angry, though he may not know why. The woman herself is, in her own mind, trying to be helpful, but the animus has taken over and instead of a statement related to this individual man and his need, the animus has answered with a generalization.

If a man said such a thing to a woman, it would no doubt come across to a woman in a preachy, superior masculine way. She would probably feel rejected and put down by the man's sweeping generalization that seems to leave her and her feelings out of the picture. Men are prone to just such sweeping statements, and the animus acts the same way. A man who wishes to relate must learn to temper his masculine judgments with eros, which always makes things personal and individual, just as a woman who remains true to her eros principle will not want to allow the animus and his sweeping statements to take over.

The animus often keeps other people from reaching and experiencing the warm, feeling side of a woman because they cannot get through the animus and his opinions. Children with such a woman for a mother feel deprived of their mother's affection because they keep coming up against the animus. She comes across to them as a hard disciplinarian, and the critical, judgmental attitudes of the animus effectively shut them out from her tenderness and affection. (The situation is exacerbated when the father has relinquished the masculine role of disciplinarian and forced the mother to assume this role in the family.) It is not that the mother does not have warm feelings for her children; they are there, but the children do not receive them because the animus blocks them. Such women may appear hard and steely, and other people may be leery of them, for their animus can wound; however, strangely enough, they themselves easily get their feelings

hurt, and when this happens they are terribly injured and bewil-
dered and do not understand why other people do not love them.
The animus-ridden woman and the martyred woman are not far
from each other.

Emily Bronte's profound novel *Wuthering Heights* is filled
with illustrations of the psychology of the animus, as Barbara
Hannah has shown in her brilliant book *Striving Towards Wholeness.*[10] Hannah points out a scene in the opening part of the novel, in which Mr. Lockwood has a vivid nightmare of the Reverend Jabes Branderham, as a good portrayal of what C. G. Jung
once called "the ravings of the animus." Mr. Lockwood, an unwelcome visitor to the austere home of the somber Heathcliff, is
forced to spend the night in Wuthering Heights because of a vio-
lent snowstorm. He is ushered by the servant into the forbidding,
gloomy room that once was used by the now-deceased Cathy, but
has remained unused for many years. Here he finally manages to
fall asleep in spite of the grim surroundings, but is awakened in
the middle of the night by a terrible nightmare. In his dream a
character appears called the Reverend Jabes Branderham, a
name Lockwood had chanced upon in some reading shortly before going to sleep. In his dream Mr. Lockwood sits imprisoned
in the midst of a somber congregation listening to the Reverend
Jabes Branderham preach an interminable sermon on the seven-
ty-times-seven sins. One by one the preacher wearisomely goes
through each of the 490 sins. Every one of these discourses is
equal to an ordinary sermon, and the sins were "of a curious
sort," "odd transgressions," Lockwood notes, "that I never
imagined previously."

"Oh, how weary I grew. How I writhed, and yawned, and
nodded, and revived! How I pinched and pricked myself, and
rubbed my eyes, and stood up, and sat down." Finally Branderham finishes with the four hundred and ninetieth sin, but then
begins the four hundred and ninety-first sin! That is too much for
Mr. Lockwood. He leaps to his feet in the dream and objects:
"Sir, . . . I have endured and forgiven the four hundred and ninety heads of your discourse. . . . The four hundred and ninety first

[10]Barbara Hannah, *Striving Towards Wholeness* (New York: G. P. Putnam's Sons, 1971), chap. 10.

is too much!" The interminable preacher is not dissuaded. Pointing his finger at Lockwood he calls on the congregation to "execute upon him the judgment." The result is pandemonium as the people rush upon Lockwood, he defends himself, and finally wakens with everyone fighting furiously with everyone else.[11]

As Barbara Hannah notes, the Reverend Jabes Branderham is an apt personification of the capacity of the animus to go on and on reciting the list of "sins" that he claims people have committed. The negative animus can dredge up the most remarkable incidents to add to his unending list of sins and failures, and in addition to acting as prosecutor, appoints himself judge as well. He has no mercy in his pronouncements, and there is no end to the list of faults he can find. Small wonder he can impart such feelings of guilt, defeat, and inferiority in people!

It is helpful to have Emily Brontë personify for us the workings of the animus in her image of the Reverend Jabes Branderham, for the term animus is a stiff term that, while scientifically useful, does not fit very well with the way he is actually experienced. When he is seen working within a woman's psyche, it is often better to speak of him as the Great Prosecutor, the Top Sergeant, the Great Scorekeeper, the Inner Judge, or, as one woman once put it, the "Duty Demon."

There are certain words of which the animus is particularly fond—"should" is perhaps the most important of these—and there are certain statements he makes more often than others. For instance, "You are no good . . . You can't do anything right . . . Other people are better than you . . . You are a failure." The differentiation of the animus is helped when a woman can recognize these autonomous thoughts that suddenly appear in her mind, sense that they are presented to her from a force within herself, and stop to question them. In many cases it helps to write them down so they can be looked at more objectively and seen for what they are. She can even put quotation marks around them because they are thoughts that act as though someone else within her mind has spoken them.

The animus can also fill a woman's mind with a strange kind

---

[11] Emily Brontë, *Wuthering Heights* (New York: Random House edition, 1943), p. 14.

of logic. A young woman who had a loving relationship with an airplane pilot was troubled one night by a dark fantasy in which her only brother was committing suicide. A train of thought then began to run through her mind that went like this: "You see how much you love your brother, yet he might die. Now if you really love your brother, your father, and your mother, you will want to go and be with them as much as possible because they may all die. And if you really love your man you will want to be with him too as much as possible. So you should give up your job, and travel wherever he goes and be with him on as many flights and overnight stops as possible because that is what you should do if you love someone." Fortunately, this "logic" was so outrageous the woman *knew* something was wrong with it. As she expressed it, "But I would not be myself if I were doing that." This illustrates the way the animus manifests himself in an autonomous train of thought, and a woman needs to be careful and not let it run her life.

This quasi-logical aspect of the animus is one reason it is so irritating to other people. His judgments, conclusions, and criticisms have a peculiarly blunt, stinging quality because they are not related to the emotional reality of the situation. The animus has a way of using a sword when a lamp would be better.

When the animus utters an opinion, it is said with an air of great authority. It is like a pronouncement, and pronouncements, of course, are indisputable. This air of authority, Emma Jung suggests in her monograph *Animus and Anima*,[12] is enhanced by our present culture, which tends to overvalue everything masculine and undervalue the feminine. Masculine achievement, power, control, success, and logic are rewarded in our society by prestige, good grades in school, and generous paychecks. The feminine principle, which tends to unite and synthesize, is undervalued culturally both in men and in women. It is as though the animus were aware of this, and so his utterances are all the more authoritative, while, conversely, a woman is led to distrust her seemingly inferior and more vague feminine intuitions and feelings, even though it is these that have the truth of the matter. This is a deplorable situation, for not only does our world need

---

[12]Emma Jung, *Animus and Anima* (Zurich: Spring Publications, 1974).

more of the healing influence and wisdom of the feminine, but the woman herself is all the more victimized by animus judgments that, if left unchallenged, nullify her own deepest psychological truth.

Since the anima and animus have these peculiarly irritating effects, it is not surprising that they are inclined to quarrel with each other. A typical anima/animus quarrel can start in many different ways. A man may come home in a dark mood. He is possessed by this mood, that is, by the anima, and exudes an air of poison and gloom. Now if the man were to tell his woman what the problem is, things could take a more positive direction, but the chances are that he will say nothing about his frame of mind, but will just inflict his mood on her. Being in this mood, of course he is not related, and his woman senses this immediately, and cannot stand the lack of relationship. She finds the psychological atmosphere, and the sense of isolation, increasingly intolerable, and also wonders if somehow she is being blamed for something, for a man in the grip of the anima has a way of being vaguely reproachful of others. At this point, unless the woman is very careful, her animus may intrude. It is as though *he* does not like that man's moody anima either, and so he will pick up his sword or club and take matters into his own hands. This may be done with some kind of stinging remark, or a direct frontal assault on the man's objectionable moodiness.

Stung by the attack, the anima of the man may retaliate. Unless the man is quick to realize what is going on, and to make a conscious response to this situation, the anima will probably drop her match into the gasoline, and the result will be an eruption of affect. The man will then become irrational and fight back in a sarcastic, affect-laden way, perhaps with a personalistic attack on his wife's character, that of her mother, and anything else that can be thought of to get revenge for the wound that has just been inflicted on him. The animus then comes back in kind, and the result is an angry quarrel. It never occurs to the man, of course, that he has become possessed by a witch inside himself; to the contrary, he is quite convinced that his wife is to blame for all of this.

Or perhaps it is the woman's animus that first delivers a stinging remark or irritating opinion. The man is immediately affected by this, but unless he is quick to realize what is happening, it is his anima who reacts. As Jung once wrote, ". . . no man can converse with an animus for five minutes without becoming the victim of his own anima . . . the animus draws his sword of power and the anima ejects her poison of illusion and seduction."[13]

At this point projections occur again, but it is not the positive animus and anima who are projected onto the human partners, creating an air of fascination and magical attraction; it is the negative images, which have the effect of driving the man and the woman apart. The man's wife now receives the projection of his inner witch, and is, accordingly, held responsible for his bad mood, while the woman projects onto her man all the infuriating qualities that, in fact, belong to the man inside of herself.

Clearly such anima/animus fights can be destructive. The tragedy is that while the man and woman have their unproductive quarrel, and the atmosphere becomes darker and darker, neither realizes that the scene is being dominated by the Invisible Partners. It is not John and Mary who are quarreling, but these archetypal figures within them. For just as the anima and animus can fall in love, so they can quarrel, and the intensity of their attraction to each other is matched only by the intensity of their dislike.

This destructive anima/animus fight is not to be confused with a genuine encounter between the actual man and woman. When John and Mary confront each other to express their anger and work out their differences, something positive can emerge. Such encounters between a man and a woman can have great psychological value and must not be avoided just because a person is too squeamish to get into emotionally difficult situations. But when John and Mary are eclipsed by their anima and animus, and *these* two begin to quarrel, the result is most unfortunate.

The strange thing is, as suggested earlier, that the quarrel could be avoided if the man would just say what it is that he is feeling, and the woman would say what it is that is troubling her. If the man directly expresses his hurt, anger, or bewilderment, it is *he* who is talking. If he does not, however, the anima gets hold

[13] Jung, *CW* 9, 2, p. 15.

of it and expresses his emotional reaction for him in the devious, destructive ways described. She exaggerates, as Jung said. In her grasp, a relatively minor personal injury becomes magnified and a mountain is made of a molehill. She falsifies. Once the personal slight or hurt is in her grasp, the facts of the situation become distorted. In the ensuing argument, what really happened becomes obscured by the emotionality of the anima. She intensifies, so that the original emotion the man felt now becomes a powerful affect, and the small fire a large one. And she mythologizes. When things are left in her hands, an ordinary human woman becomes a goddess or a witch and an ordinary human situation takes on a highly dramatic character.

Similarly, when a woman who is troubled by something in a personal relationship says what she feels, it is she who is speaking, and the matter can be worked out. But if she hides her true feelings, it is the animus who seizes his club or sword and tries to set matters straight. The result is disastrous as far as the relationship is concerned, and is a defeat for the woman's ego, for the ego always experiences defeat when it becomes possessed by the anima or animus. Club in hand, the animus will let the offending man have it by some form of direct attack that may have little perceivable relationship to the actual offense. Taking his sword of seeming logic, the animus will bring up some argument that has little or nothing to do with the real emotional issue. Irritated at such an irrational assault, and frustrated by its seeming unfairness, a man is all too likely to fall into the clutches of his anima at this point and then dark things happen.

A woman can avoid this by saying something like, "You seem to be upset about something. Are you angry at me?" If he is angry at her, he can say so and perhaps the matter can be resolved. If not, the woman need not feel guilty or anxious, and can afford to let her man remain with his mood and work it out himself while she goes about her business. For it is not her job to get him out of his mood; that is a task that every man must take on himself. Of course the man may be dishonest. He may snarl, "No!" when he really means yes. It is probably best, however, for the woman to take his words at face value and let him stew in his own juice, and say to herself, "Okay, he said I was not to blame for his bad mood so I accept no guilt or responsibility for what he is feeling." It goes without saying, of course, that if people persist in emotional dishonesty with each other, relationship is exceedingly difficult.

A man who is confronted by a woman's animus can help the situation by keeping his cool and responding out of his own masculine strength. If a man's masculinity is stronger than that of the animus, he can usually free the woman from possession; at least he can keep himself from falling into the clutches of his inner woman. It usually helps to find out what the problem really is. "What is really bothering you?" a man might ask if he realizes he has just been attacked by a woman's animus. He may often find that what really is bothering her has nothing to do with the subject the animus has brought up. (It isn't that she doesn't like the suit he has put on, which she has chosen to violently criticize, but that she is hurt because he ignored her at the party the night before.)

In her masterful book *The Feminine in Fairy Tales,* Marie-Louise von Franz stresses the role of hurt feelings in animus attacks by women. If one is upset or possessed by a mood, she points out, "It is very helpful to ask, 'Where have I been disappointed or hurt in my feelings and have not sufficiently noticed it?'" She continues:

> Then you will frequently find the cause. If you can get back to the origin of the hurt and where you have not worked it out, the animus possession will walk out; for that is where it jumped in, and that is why in animus possession there is always an undertone of the reproachful woman.
>
> Animus possession in a woman annoys men madly; they go up in the air at once. But what really gets the man's goat is the undertone of *lamenting reproachfullness.* Men who know a little more about this know that eighty-five percent of animus possession is a disguised appeal for love, although unfortunately it has the wrong effect, since it chases away the thing that is wanted. Underneath the animus there is a feeling of reproach and at the same time of wanting to get back at the one who has hurt you. It is a vicious circle and arguing develops into a typical animus scene.[14]

---

[14] Von Franz, *The Feminine in Fairy Tales,* p. 27. Italics mine.

It is important to add, however, that much the same thing can be said of a man. If he falls into a mood, he can often free himself by asking, "Where did something go wrong? What does my inner woman not like? Did something that was done or said hurt my feelings?" If we can get to the origin of the hurt and do something about it, the anima possession will disappear. Men in such a mood also exude the atmosphere of the "reproachful hurt woman," for that is what the anima can be like, and that is why it is so essential for a man to become conscious of his feelings and to act on them.

A man must overcome his fears of rejection for, as noted before, many men fear a woman's anger because they are afraid of her rejection. In an effort to avoid the emotional trauma of rejection a man may do all the wrong things, such as trying to appease the woman's animus, or giving in to a woman's more childish reactions, or arguing her out of her complaints. If he does any of these, he never gets to the bottom of the matter; by his weak and defensive posture he does his woman a great disservice, for what she needs from him is his strength and willingness to get to the root of the matter.

As we have seen, beneath such emotional insecurity in a man may be his inner little boy who fears mother's rejection, and who cannot stand being left out in the cold. There may even be deep-rooted memories of a mother who once tried to control him by rejection, saying, in effect, "If you do not do what I want, I will treat you coldly and shut you out, and you will not be able to stand that." He may also recall his mother's use of guilt as a mechanism of control and punishment. "You are a bad boy, you have made mother angry, and I will shut you up in your room." This may be a memory silently at work in the man's fearful response to his wife, for as far as men are concerned, women have a powerful guilt-producing mechanism, which is both feared and hated. Many men, out of sheer inability to face this guilt, either quit the field in the face of an angry woman, or find some way to keep her down so they can remain top dog. So in learning to relate to a woman, a man also has to come to terms with the little boy in himself.

It can be seen that in working out a relationship a person

must also work things out within himself or herself; also one must learn that being a partner in a relationship is extremely important. As Jung once put it, "One is always in the dark about one's own personality. One needs others to get to know oneself."[15]

One word of caution: In discussing their relationship a man and woman do well to avoid the use of the terms anima and animus, or any psychological terms for that matter. It is best to use ordinary language, for the use of psychological language is unnatural in relationships and tends to depersonalize them. The value of being aware of the anima and animus is that *we* may know what is going on, and our heightened consciousness helps us in working out the relationship, but the use of psychological language as we do so is generally destructive. So a woman who sees her man in a mood, instead of saying, "Looks like you are gripped by your anima," might say, "You look upset; is something bothering you?" And a man, suspecting his woman's animus is attacking him, can say, "I have a feeling that you are angry at me about something," instead of saying, "Your animus is showing again."

A final comment on the way the anima and animus may negatively affect our lives concerns the influence they have on our choice of marriage partners. Because these figures so readily project themselves onto members of the opposite sex, and tend to possess us to the extent that we are unaware of them, they often have a determinative influence upon the kind of man or woman who becomes our husband or wife. An anima-possessed man, with a weak ego and a powerful witchlike anima figure, will quite likely unconsciously select a domineering animus-ridden woman. In this he acts out his inner situation in his outer relationship. Conversely, a woman who is dominated from within by a negative, defeating animus may very likely wind up with a man who portrays this negative animus for her by putting her down, negating and criticizing her. This explains some of the unlikely unions that are made between men and women, and also shows that truly we have no free choice unless we are psychologically conscious persons.

---

[15] *Jung Speaking*, p. 165.

In one of Jung's letters there is an interesting story that illustrates this. A man who had a gift for writing, but had done nothing with it, had three marriages. His first wife was a pianist, who left him after a marriage of seventeen years; the second was an artist whose death ended twenty-two years of an "idyllic" marriage; the third was an actress. After the death of the second wife he experienced strange psychological phenomena, such as hearing "raps and taps" in the bedroom, about two or three times a week. In his letter Jung tells the man that his choice of wives was influenced by the anima. The man had a creative gift, but not the necessary talent to express it adequately, so he did not live his own creative side; he projected it onto the creative women he married. In this way he missed part of his own life, and it was the unused creativity in himself that was behind the strange psychological phenomena. Jung commented, "In practice it means that the woman of your choice represents your own task you did not understand."[16] The same thing could be said of the choice every man and woman makes of his or her partner in life; in some way the partner represents something we need to understand about ourselves.

Of course this is just one level of relationship; relationship has many meanings and many levels. The point I wish to make is that the Invisible Partners add an often overlooked level or dimension to our choice of partners in life.

I have talked of the negative side of the anima and animus. It is always best to get the bad news first; besides, it is usually this negative side that we experience first. But the anima and animus also have a positive aspect, in fact, when they are in their correct place they have a great blessing to give to us. However, in order to realize this blessing we must be able to overcome their negative effects. In the next chapter I will suggest how we can do this, and then go on to discuss the positive nature of these figures.

---

[16] C. G. Jung, *Letters Vol. 2* (Princeton, N.J.: Princeton University Press, 1975), p. 321.

Chapter Three

In Goethe's great drama *Faust,* when Mephistopheles is asked who he is, the devil replies, "A part of that power which always wills the evil and always works the good."[1] So it is that the power of evil, while striving to bring about destruction, can in fact engender the good.

It has been demonstrated that the anima and animus have their dark side, and can destroy people if they are allowed to possess them with their dark rages and negative thoughts. But a potential for the light lies hidden even in this darkness.

Robert Johnson gives us a good example of this in his masterful book *HE!,* a psychological study of the meaning of the legend of the Holy Grail. It seems that Parsifal, the hero of the tale, has risen to the top of the heap in his knightly world. He has slain more knights than anyone else, done more great deeds, achieved more fame. So a feast is given in his honor, and he, and all the other knights of the Round Table, are congratulating themselves on what splendid fellows they are, when in walks a horrible looking woman, so ugly that she is called the "hideous damsel." "Her black hair was tressed in two braids, iron dark were her hands and nails. Her closed eyes small like a rat's. Her

---

[1] Goethe's *Faust,* by C. F. MacIntyre (Norfolk, Conn.: New Directions, 1941), part 1, p. 91.

nose like an ape and cat. Her lips like an ass and bull. Bearded was she, humped breast and back, her loins and shoulders twisted like roots of a tree. Never in royal court was such a damsel seen."[2] So the legend describes this terrifying feminine apparition. The mere sight of her casts a pall on the knightly company. The feasting and self-congratulating stop, a hush comes over everyone, and then the hideous damsel begins a recitation of Parsifal's sins. On she goes about the failures of his life, the damsels he has left weeping, the children who have been orphaned because of him, and when she is through she says, "It is all your fault."[3]

Of course the hideous damsel is a personification of the anima. Experientially she would be felt as a terrible mood, a foreboding depression and great malaise, which might overcome a man at just the point when he is at the apex of his masculine career in the world. As Johnson points out, the hideous damsel is a personification of that kind of male depression which typically comes in middle age at just the point when a man has reached his greatest strengths and successes. She personifies "the anima gone absolutely sour and dark." She is the living image of the man's failure to deal with the other side of his life—the feminine side, the spiritual side, the soul side. She is dark and monstrous in direct proportion to the man's outer success, and inner denial of the things of his soul.

On the surface of it, the hideous damsel looks as though she came straight from hell. In fact, she can be a hellish force in a man, pulling him into depression, drink, illness, and suicide. But curiously enough in the legend of Parsifal she has a most salutary effect, for, because of her, Parsifal, who is destined to find the Holy Grail, symbol of wholeness and completeness, resumes the spiritual journey that he had abandoned earlier in his masculine urge for adventure, conquest, and worldly success.

As Robert Johnson points out, when the hideous damsel looms up in a man's psychology, it is essential that the man respond to her correctly. If he does, she becomes the instrument for setting him on his right path again; if he makes the wrong re-

---

[2] Robert Johnson, *HE!* (King of Prussia, Pa.: Religious Publishing Company, 1974), p. 74.
[3] Ibid., p. 75.

sponse, she becomes the instrument of his destruction. The wrong response would be trying to avoid her, that is, avoiding the meaning of his depression by one of a thousand tricks: still more extraverted activities and plans for outer success, drinking, drugs, exchanging one woman for another. These are all typical ways that men have of avoiding the hideous damsel and keeping their life energies going as before. In so doing they simply heap psychological sin on psychological sin and turn the anima still more against them. But if a man will accept his dark moods as a call to find his soul, and complete his journey to become a whole person, the anima changes and becomes his ally.

Much the same thing sometimes happens to women when they reach those mysterious and difficult middle years of life. At this point in her life a woman may have fulfilled earlier feminine goals. She has her husband, her home, and her children, who are now grown or nearly grown. But instead of being content she may become depressed and feel unfulfilled. The problem lies with the animus, who is now acting like a devil, and is telling her that everything she has done so far in life adds up to nothing, or, speaking through her mouth, he bores other people to distraction with banal generalizations. If she is not to fall under the domination of this devil, she must undergo a journey for spiritual life and development. There are no choices: Either she develops now in a new way, and expands into the world of logos, spirit, and mind, or she falls more and more under the domination of an animus figure who has turned peevish and cruel.

So while there is a dark side to the anima and animus it would seem as though it is this dark side that can set us on our path to wholeness again. The dark, negative side of these inner figures becomes greater the more it is ignored. We help ourselves best when we turn *toward* the anima and animus, not away from them, and undergo a new psychological development that will take them into account. For a man, this may mean a renewed respect for the world of the heart, for relationships, for the soul, and for the search for meaning. For a woman this may mean a renewed journey into the world of spirit, of understanding, and a new kind of involvement with the world beyond the family. Thus even the dark sides of the Invisible Partners seem to serve the purposes of life. Of course the stakes are high. To ignore them, or to fail to understand what is required of us, will have undesirable results, but, conversely, to recognize the reality of these inner figures, and to go in the direction in which they point, is to be on the path to a new development.

The first step in freeing oneself from the negative effects of the anima and animus is to recognize the problem. For a man, this means recognizing that his moods, compulsive sexual fantasies, and insatiable restlessness have this dark feminine figure as their source. For a woman it means recognizing that the opinions and destructive criticisms that suddenly come into her consciousness have the inner figure of the animus behind them. For both men and women, of course, it means withdrawing the projections of these figures from actual human beings.

Projections are integrated by being made conscious. As we have suggested earlier, we cannot keep projections from occurring; they happen quite spontaneously and are not subject to our conscious control. But we can learn to recognize that a projection has occurred; whenever a man or woman fascinates us we can be sure that a projected content of the unconscious is at work. In their all-too-human reality people are not fascinating; it is the archetypal figures of the unconscious that are fascinating. Recognizing fascinating projections when they occur makes it possible for us to become aware of the anima/animus figures who stand behind these projections.

In fact, this may be what the anima and animus want. It is as though they project themselves outside of us onto suitable people because they want to be recognized, and that is the only way they can reach us. As already noted, the most common way for the anima to claim a man's attention is to fill his mind with a powerful sexual-erotic fantasy, and, similarly, it is the animus who lies behind many a woman's sexual-erotic fantasy about a man. It is as though the inner figures are trying in this way to get our attention.

Once the anima and animus are recognized, a great work of psychological differentiation of the personality can begin. For instance, a man can begin to separate his moods from his feelings. His moods are from the anima; the feelings are his own. As we have seen, if a man expresses his feelings in relationship, he does not fall into moods. So, to free himself from the clutches of his anima, a man must learn to relate to his feelings, and to express them in human relationships when the situation calls for it. In this way he comes out of the Mother and develops his eros side. Again we see the odd fact: The anima, who can be so negative, facilitates a man's psychological development when he takes her into account; because of her a man is forced to become conscious of his affective side.

Similarly with the animus. In order to fight against the negative judgments of the animus, a woman must come to know and value what is truly important to her. When the animus says that this or that is of no value, the woman needs to recognize these thoughts and challenge them. She needs to find her own ground and stand firmly on it, to value her feminine feelings and eros and not allow the animus, with his sweeping condemnations, to rob her of her self-value. In accomplishing this task, a woman may, for the first time, discover what is truly important to her.

As we have seen, the negative animus resembles an inferior, ill-informed, and prejudiced man; his sweeping judgments and banal opinions come from his ignorance. So a woman may need to sit down with her animus and say, "This is the way it is, and this is what is important to me. You are not to keep telling me to the contrary." Obviously, in order to do this she must first know what is important to her. In this way, the animus can have the positive effect of helping a woman become conscious of her true values.

She must also find out what *he* wants. As we noted, the anima and animus live through us, and the lives we lead must have room in them for these archetypal figures and their life energy. For a man this means that his life must include warm and meaningful human relationships, and the area of the heart, for the anima and the feminine always stand on the side of a man's heart. For a woman this means that her life must include a certain fulfillment in the area of goals, aspirations, spirit, and mind.

When we talk with the anima and animus we must regard them as the autonomous psychological realities that they are. Indeed, working with them requires us to overcome what C. G. Jung once called the "monotheism of consciousness," and recognize that our personalities are made up not only of consciousness, but of a multitude of lesser or partial personalities as well.

A great darkness exists today in this regard, for we persist in the belief that only the ego and its world exist, in spite of the evidence all around us that human beings are readily possessed by they-know-not-what within them. Jung wrote, "we lack knowledge of the unconscious psyche and pursue the cult of consciousness to the exclusion of all else. Our true religion is a monotheism of consciousness, . . . coupled with a fanatical denial that there are parts of the psyche which are autonomous."[4]

It is because the psyche is made up of these autonomous, partial personalities that it is possible to talk to oneself. This is not an indication that one is crazy; it is just the opposite, for the more one comes into a conscious relationship with the different parts of oneself the more there is promoted from within a synthesis and harmonization of the personality. A man who wishes to talk with his anima might begin by addressing himself to a mood that has engulfed him and from which he cannot extricate himself. This can be done by personifying the mood in his imagination and talking to it. This is not difficult because most psychic contents, especially the anima and the animus, appear in a personified form in our dreams and fantasies. What would you like to say to a mood that has engulfed you and will not go away? Whatever that might be, write it down, just as though you were writing to an actual person. Then imagine what that personified mood would say in response. Whatever comes into your mind would be the reply. Do not stop to question whether or not this is "legitimate," but simply write down what the personified mood says. This may call forth another response from you, with a second reply from the personified mood, and so a dialogue ensues. The value of writing down the dialogue is that it gives it reality, makes a record of the conversation that can be referred to later, and strengthens the hand of the ego in its dealings with the powerful feminine numen.[5]

In actual practice, an anima mood is usually quite willing to

---

[4] *Secret of the Golden Flower*, p. 111.

[5] This technique of dialoguing with the anima or animus is part of what C. G. Jung called "active imagination." Jung has described this method of relating to the unconscious in various places. See also the Appendix on active imagination at the back of this book.

talk. It resembles a woman who responds positively to a move toward relationship from her man, but becomes dark and unpleasant when ignored. It is characteristic of the feminine to want attention and to resent being ignored. Indeed, one begins to feel
that the fantastic and dangerous machinations of the anima are
designed from the beginning for the sole purpose of getting the
man's attention, and compelling him to relate to her as his inner
woman or soul. When this is done, as we shall see, the negative
effects of the anima begin to give way, and the positive manifestations tend to appear.

Dialoguing with the animus is as natural as with the anima.
The former tends to be more verbal, and is usually recognized at
first as autonomous thoughts appearing in a woman's mind.
When a woman begins to recognize that these thoughts come
from the animus and not from her ego, she begins to make the
important distinction between herself and the male factor within
her. Sometimes it helps to start by carefully noting the kinds of
things the animus is saying, usually characterized, as we have
seen, by "shoulds" and "oughts" and judgments of one sort or another. As suggested in chapter two, it often helps to write these
down and put quotation marks around them to emphasize the
fact that these do not represent a woman's own thinking but the
opinions of the animus. Then it is only a simple step beyond this
for a woman to reply to the voice of the animus. In this way she
can challenge his opinions, disagree with him, and educate him
about her true feelings and the actual situation. Writing down the
ensuing dialogue strengthens a woman's ego, for taking up pen or
pencil to write is the ego's work. Once such a dialogue is begun,
the animus may go on to tell a woman what it is that *he* really
wants out of life. When this happens the chances for a positive relationship between a woman and her animus are greatly increased.

The key word in coming to terms with the anima and the
animus is *relationship*. Anima and animus are archetypal figures,
which means they do not simply go away and disappear from
one's life, but act like permanent partners with whom we must
find some way of relating no matter how difficult they may be.
But relationship makes all the difference. When a figure of the
unconscious is denied, rejected, or ignored, it turns against us

and shows its negative side. When it is accepted, understood, and related to, its positive side tends to appear.

But at the same time that a man learns to dialogue with the anima, and a woman with the animus, men and women must also learn to dialogue with each other. It should be obvious by now that a relationship with a member of the opposite sex is of great value in working out the anima and animus problem, and, conversely, that a good rapport with our anima and animus is of great value in woking out our human relationships. Just as a dialogue with the anima or animus will help us to distinguish what belongs to the ego and what belongs to the unconscious figures, so a dialogue with the man or woman in our life will help us to understand and appreciate our differences and each other's true personality. Only through dialogue can two human beings begin to see their own, and the other person's, reality. Such dialogue, which consists of stating in one way or another one's own feelings and thoughts, and then listening carefully to what the other person is saying, is greatly facilitated when the anima and animus are out of the picture. If these Invisible Partners are intruding into the sphere of the relationship, then moods, affects, opinions, and judgments will cloud the atmosphere, leading to distortions, recriminations, and the kind of anima/animus quarrel that has been described.

So if a man wishes to come to a rapprochement with his feminine side he also needs to understand the personality of the important woman in his life, and a woman, conversely, needs to understand her man and his thoughts and feelings. Men and women think and feel differently; their mental processes are not alike and a relationship between the sexes requires that we understand the differences that separate us. When we do there are salutary results, one of which is a broadening of consciousness. When a man understands something of a woman, his masculine consciousness is expanded and his personality enriched. This broadening of consciousness defeats the negative aspects of the anima and animus and puts these inner partners in their psychologically correct place, which Jung repeatedly tells us is *within* and not without.

This brings us to another of Jung's definitions of the anima and animus: They personify the collective unconscious, and therefore their true psychological purpose is to be a function of relationship between the ego and the collective unconscious, to build a bridge, as it were, between the world of consciousness and the world of inner images.

This is Jung's most common definition of the anima and animus. He offers it to us in one of his earliest studies, in which he says that the function of the animus (and the same would be true of the anima) "is . . . to facilitate relations with the unconscious."[6] And in his commentary on the ancient Chinese book *The Secret of the Golden Flower* he said, "I have defined the anima in man as a personification of the unconscious in general, and have therefore taken it to be a bridge to the unconscious, that is, to be a function of relationship to the unconscious."[7] It also occurs in *Man and His Symbols*, in which Jung's colleague and disciple Marie-Louise von Franz states, "The anima is a personification of all feminine psychological tendencies in a man's psyche, such as vague feelings and moods, . . . and . . . his *relation to the unconscious*."[8]

Practically speaking, this means that if a man will look at what lies behind his moods, affects, fantasies, and emotions, those spontaneous psychic events which form the background to his consciousness and which the anima brings to him, he will arrive at what is going on in his unconscious personality. It is as though the anima becomes contaminated with everything within a man which wants to reach consciousness. Consequently, if a man can take the anima as an inner figure, he arrives at those archetypal images which form the foundation of his personality.

This is difficult for modern man to understand because we do not take the reality of the inner world seriously; in fact, most people have no idea that there is an inner world. Since we have no inkling of the inner world, the highly personified figures of the anima and animus appear to us on the outside, where they complicate relationships and create illusions, in the projected manner discussed, and begin to malfunction by creating moods and generating opinions.

---

[6] Jung, *CW* 7, p. 207.
[7] Jung, *The Secret of the Golden Flower*, p. 119.
[8] Jung, *Man and His Symbols*, p. 177. Italics mine.

An evil condition develops when any part of an organism fails to perform its proper role, and instead usurps a role that does not belong to it. For instance, the intellect becomes evil if, instead of serving the whole person by performing its particular function of discrimination, it usurps the wholeness of the personality by dominating and excluding other aspects of the psyche. So the anima and animus also become embroiled with evil when they are not in the correct place. Jung wrote, "The reason for this perversion is clearly the failure to give adequate recognition to an inner world which stands autonomously opposed to the outer world, and makes just as serious demands on our capacity for adaptation."[9]

To perceive the reality of the anima and animus thus requires considerable conscious effort, which is why Jung referred to the encounter with the anima or animus as the "master piece" of individuation.[10] In the first place, we must overcome the tendency to think of ourselves as exclusively masculine or feminine; for many people this in itself represents a revolution in thinking. But then we must go further and realize that our conscious life rests on the vast sea of an inner world of which we know very little. We must realize that this inner world is as real and as objective to our conscious standpoint as is the outer world of physical reality, for this dimension of the unconscious would exist whether we existed or not, just as the outer world exists whether or not a given human individual exists. It is this objectively real inner world that Jung calls the collective unconscious; it would have been called the spiritual world by early Christians, or personified as a mythological world of spirit beings by the American Indians. It is also this world to which the anima and animus can relate us when they have been withdrawn from projections in the outer world and taken back into our inner world.

When the anima functions in her correct place, she serves to broaden and enlarge a man's consciousness, and to enrich his personality by infusing into him, through dreams, fantasies, and inspired ideas, an awareness of an inner world of psychic images and life-giving emotions. A man's consciousness tends to be too

---

[9] Jung, *CW* 7, p. 208.
[10] Jung, *CW* 9, 1, p. 29.

focused and concentrated; it easily becomes rigid and constricted, and, without contact with the unconscious, becomes dry and sterile. Jung wrote, "If the products of the anima (dreams, fantasies, visions, symptoms, chance ideas, etc.) are assimilated, digested, and integrated, this has a beneficial effect on the growth and development . . . of the psyche."[11]

Masculine consciousness has been likened to the sun, and feminine consciousness to the moon. At noon everything is seen in bright outline and one thing is clearly differentiated from another. But no one can stand too much of this hot, bright sun. Without the cool, the moist, the dark, the landscape soon becomes unbearable, and the earth dries up and will not produce life. That is the way a man's life becomes without the fertilizing influence on him of the feminine. Without a relationship to his inner world, a man can focus, but lacks imagination; he can pursue goals, but lacks emotion; he can strive for power, but is unable to be creative because he cannot produce new life out of himself. Only the fruitful joining of the Yin principle to the Yang principle can stir up his energies, can prevent his consciousness from becoming sterile, and his masculine power from drying up.

So the anima mediates to a man invaluable psychological qualities that make him alive. For this reason, at various times Jung has also defined the anima as "the archetype of life," and once said that she is "an allurement to the intensification of life."[12] She is like soul to a man, that elusive but vital ingredient that alone makes life worth living and gives to a man a sense of something worth striving for. It is the anima who gives a man *heart*, enabling him to be strong of heart and courageous in the face of life's burdens and afflictions.

As the archetype of life, the anima contains the element of meaning. It is not that she has the answers; rather, she embodies within herself the secret of life, and helps a man discover it by leading him to a knowledge of his own soul. "Something strangely meaningful clings to her." Jung wrote, "a secret knowledge or hidden wisdom, which contrasts most curiously with her irra-

---

[11] C. G. Jung, *CW* 14, *Mysterium Coniunctionis*; (Princeton, N.J.: Princeton University Press, 1963; 2nd printing 1974), p. 308.

[12] Jung, *Letters* 2, p. 423.

tional elfin nature." And, he added, when a man comes to grips with the anima he comes to realize that "behind all her cruel sporting with human fate there lies something like a hidden purpose which seems to reflect a superior knowledge of life's laws. . . . And the more this meaning is recognized, the more the anima loses her impetuous and compulsive character."[13] As a personification of life, the anima personifies for a man "the life behind consciousness that cannot be completely integrated with it, but from which . . . consciousness arises," and "it is always the *a priori* element in (a man's) moods, reactions, impulses, and whatever else is spontaneous in psychic life."[14]

We must not, however, think that the anima is "good." The anima is neither good nor bad; she just *is*. She wants life, and so she seems to want both good and bad, or, rather, she is not concerned with these moral categories. That is why working with the anima is always a delicate matter. One can no more deliver oneself over to the anima lock stock and barrel than one can surrender the whole of oneself to any particular psychological function or quality. It is also the anima who seems to arouse a man's capacity for love. When we first fall in love we are flooded with powerful, life-giving emotions. This is why the anima can best be described poetically and not scientifically, dramatically and not concretely. Yet, as we have seen, a man's relationship with her must develop beyond the mere sensation of falling or being in love, as he must come to perceive that the life-giving feminine soul is within himself. He cannot afford to let his anima live only in projection onto a woman, but must reach beyond this projection to search for the soul within himself. Jung said, in a letter to a woman who was carrying a man's projected soul image for him, "Since he is unable to see you as a real woman behind his projection, you seem to be a 'sphinx.' In reality his soul is his sphinx, and he should try to solve the riddle."[15]

It is not, however, that the anima does the loving inside of a man. She is not identical with his eros, but arouses his eros. She awakens in a man his capacity for love and personal relationship,

---

[13] Jung, *CW* 9, 1, pp. 30 and 31.
[14] Ibid., p. 27.
[15] Jung, *Letters* 2, p. 402.

but she is not that love and personal relationship. It is the man who loves and feels, not his anima, though she may be likened to the spark that ignites his flame.

This last point is one that James Hillman takes up in his two articles on the anima in the 1973 and 1974 issues of *Spring*. Jung often referred to the anima as though she were identical with eros, and many Jungian analysts speak of the anima as though she were identical with feeling, as if feeling and eros were necessarily feminine and not masculine. Yet the Greek god Eros is himself a masculine deity, even though he is Aphrodite's son, and there is no good reason for ascribing feeling only to the feminine. It seems more accurate to say that the anima is a function that arouses and constellates eros in a man, but that there is such a thing as masculine eros as well as feminine eros. That is a way of saying that it is the man himself who loves, even though the feminine may arouse his love. In the same way, there is no good reason for identifying the anima with feeling, or the animus with thinking. A man can feel, and a woman can think, although the anima and the animus may arouse, aid, and direct these functions.

Another point of confusion in this regard is whether or not there is any such thing as "anima development." Jungians often speak of anima development in a man as though it were the man's task to "develop his anima" so he could relate, feel, and love more deeply. Jung himself speaks of four stages of the anima: as Eve, as Helen of Troy, as the Virgin Mary, and as Sophia. The first, Eve, is anima on the lowest, biological level, as the source of instinct and the instigator of sexuality. As Helen of Troy the anima personifies beauty and the soul, and is no longer completely equated with instinctuality. As the Virgin Mary she personifies the possibility of relationship with God, and as Sophia she embodies the principle of relationship to the highest wisdom.[16]

Undoubtedly the anima can appear on many different levels; the question is whether it is the anima who develops or the man who develops. The Greeks spoke of Aphrodite Pandemos and

[16] C. G. Jung, *CW* 16, *The Practice of Psychotherapy* (New York: Pantheon Books, 1954, revised and augmented 1966), p. 174.

Aphrodite Ouranos. The former was "Aphrodite for everyone" and the latter was the "heavenly or spiritual Aphrodite." Aphrodite Pandemos would be Aphrodite as experienced on the level of sexual, instinctual union. Experienced in this way, Aphrodite would personify the anima as she appears in sexual erotic fantasies and instinctual urges. But the spiritual Aphrodite personifies the anima as the function that relates a man's soul to God, and helps him achieve the highest possible spiritual union. However, in my view it is not the anima who undergoes a "development," but the man himself who must undergo a development. If a man's character and understanding are at a low, unconscious level, he will experience the anima on her lowest level, and not be able to understand or appreciate her higher qualities. But if the man undergoes development and acquires "soul," the anima in her highest manifestations can become meaningful to him.

Another point at issue with regard to the anima is whether she can ever be "conquered" and depersonified, or whether she always retains her elusive personified nature. Jung often spoke of the anima as though she were a being who personified herself in a most irritating way and who had to be conquered and transformed into an impersonal psychological function. For instance, in *Two Essays on Analytical Psychology* he wrote, "I recognize that there is some psychic factor (the anima) active in me which eludes my conscious will in the most incredible manner. It can put extraordinary ideas into my head, induce in me unwanted and unwelcome moods and emotions, lead me to astonishing actions for which I can accept no responsibility, upset my relations with other people in a very irritating way, etc. I feel powerless against this fact and, what is worse, I am in love with it, so that all I can do is marvel."[17]

It is perfectly true that the anima can have all of these disturbing effects on a man, yet what a man must "conquer" is himself, although this will also mean that he must not allow this beguiling and deceptive feminine creature within himself to seduce him. If he succeeds in "bottling up" the anima, that is, not allowing her to run his outer life, dominate his moods, and destroy his relationships, then, as we have seen, the anima tends to take her

---

[17] Jung, *CW* 7, pp. 225–226.

proper place as a function within him, leading him into a deeper experience of his own soul. Yet the anima seems to stubbornly resist being depersonified. She remains the personification, as Hillman puts it, of a powerful feminine numen. For this reason, Hillman sees no value in trying to break up the personifications of the anima. In fact, it is precisely because she does personify herself in our dreams and imagination that we can achieve a relatedness to her.

Moreover, Hillman points out, if we persist in trying to conquer the anima, and force her to be what we want her to be, this puts the ego in a "heroic stance," that is, reinforces a masculine stance that is certain to result in a continued devaluation of the feminine and exaggeration of the ego. Jung himself, in other places, seems to concede that the anima is irreducibly a personified figure. Of both anima and animus he wrote, "It is not we who personify them; they have a personal nature from the very beginning."[18]

The anima as the bridge between a man's consciousness and the world of the unconscious can be contrasted with the function of the persona in masculine psychology. The word *persona* means mask. It denotes the front or face that the ego presents to the outer world. The persona is thus a function of relationship between the ego and outer reality, just as the anima is the function of relationship between the ego and inner reality. The persona is a useful, even essential, psychological function. Without a certain amount of persona we can scarcely carry on in life. It is not only a mask behind which we can hide, it is also a means of adaptation to outer reality. Without any persona it would be very difficult to relate to the demands that come to us from other people, our work, and society in general. The difficulty comes when someone identifies with the persona. Then they think they *are* that front they present to the outer world, and they lose awareness of their true reality, especially of the dark, shadow side of their personality. When people identify with the persona, they are not real; they go through life with a face, but no inner depth.

The anima stands in a compensatory relationship to this per-

***

[18] C. G. Jung, *CW* 13, *Alchemical Studies;* (Princeton, N.J.: Princeton University Press, 1967, 1970 edition), par. 62.

sona. If we are too identified with it, we can expect the anima to react accordingly. Only if we have the correct relationship to the persona can we have the correct relationship to the anima. We can think, for instance, of a powerful tyrant—a Nero or a Hitler—whose mere word affects the lives of many people, and whose power in the world of outer reality leads him to believe that he is an all-powerful person. But inwardly such a man may be beset by fearsome and dark fantasies over which he has no control. His soul is possessed by frightening fears; he sees threats in every corner, and he is helpless in the presence of dark and troubling thoughts, just as King Saul was helpless in the face of his evil moods.[19]

The Roman Emperor Caligula is a good example. Caligula was so ruthless and identified with his power that he is said to have reminded guests at his banquets that he could have them all killed at any time, and is reputed to have said to his wife or mistress while embracing her, "Off comes this beautiful head whenever I give the word."[20] Yet it is also said of him that "he hid under the bed when it thundered, and fled in terror from the sight of Aetna's flames. He found it hard to sleep and would wander through his enormous palace at night crying for the dawn."[21] It is the anima who sends these troubling, fear-laden fantasies into the moods of such a man, who inspires the sleepless nights and vague feelings of foreboding, and he is as helpless in the face of them as he is all-powerful in his dealings with the outer world. In this way the anima compensates a faulty one-sidedness in his character.

Or perhaps it is a powerful business executive, whose decisions influence many, around whom obedient secretaries hover, and who is played up to by insecure subordinates. He lives in a world of tall buildings with elaborate offices, padded expense accounts, and important people on the board. Yet inwardly he may be victimized by vague fears and controlled by compulsive sexual fantasies, which may compel him to visit the pornographic movies on his way home or have call girls visit him in a motel. It is

---

[19] Cf. I Sam. 18:10–11.

[20] Suetonius, *Gaius*, quoted in Will Durant's *Caesar and Christ*, p. 226.

[21] Ibid., p. 265.

the anima who is behind these fears and fantasies, and she rules him from within as completely as he, on the outside, rules others.

It is, once again, the message of the hideous maiden, as seen in Robert Johnson's analysis of the Grail Legend. Parisfal, the great outer hero and master of the world of knights, is helpless to oppose the hideous maiden, the image of his anima, who has gone dark on him because, in his concentration on outer success, he has neglected his inner journey.

But if it appears at first as though it is the anima who is the negative figure, possessing a man with uncontrollable and unwelcome thoughts or fantasies, this is only the superficial manifestation of a much deeper problem. She really has a positive, not a negative, function, and serves to bring a man away from a path in life that is false to himself and his highest values; to lead him back to the path of wholeness and spiritual development. She is serving a constructive function, not a destructive one, and as soon as she is properly recognized and appreciated her positive aspect appears. Even in her negative aspect she remains true to herself and her basic function: the bridge to the unconscious, and to the world of a man's soul.

In his positive aspect the animus plays an indispensable role in a woman's individuation process. His main function is to be a psychopomp, a guide who leads a woman through her inner world to her soul. In dreams, the animus, as guide and creative spirit, typically appears as a gifted man, a priest, teacher, doctor, god, or a man with unusual powers. Again it is essential, if the positive aspect of the animus is to emerge, that he assume his proper function as a bridge between a woman's consciousness and her unconscious inner world; if he functions only on the outside he assumes the negative forms that have been discussed. As Jung once said, "In his real form he (the animus) is a hero, there is something divine about him" but when not in his real form he is "an opinionating substitute."[22]

The creative animus blazes a trail for a woman; he does things first that she must later undertake for herself. He leads the way, and opens up a line of development. This can sometimes be

[22] C. G. Jung, "The Interpretation of Visions," *Spring*, 1966, p. 143.

seen in a woman's dreams in which a man undertakes a journey, overcomes a danger, or endures a difficulty—a task to which the woman herself will soon be called. Jung notes, in commenting on a woman's vision in which the animus seemed to be performing a heroic function, "It is the motif we have encountered many times before: always when some new enterprise that she cannot face becomes necessary, the animus precedes her."[23]

Just as the anima often first appears to a man in projection onto an outer woman, or in the form of powerful sexual-erotic fantasies, so the animus also typically manifests himself to a woman in powerful fantasies or projections. If this numinous image is not taken psychologically, and recognized as a figure of her inner world, he readily becomes what Esther Harding called the "ghostly lover."[24] As the ghostly lover the animus haunts a woman's mind, seduces her into unreal romantic fantasies, and absorbs her consciousness more and more into unreality. No psychological development can then take place, for the woman becomes lost in love fantasies that are not related to the reality of an actual man, nor to the reality of her inner world. It is not, however, the animus who is at fault. He is trying his best to attract her attention by means of these powerful fantasies; it is the woman herself whose consciousness must develop and mature so she is capable of understanding her fantasies in the correct way. The story of Jane in the first chapter is a good illustration of the way in which the animus as ghostly lover can upset a woman's life and lead her into unreality.

In his positive aspect, the animus embodies the driving force for individuation in a woman's psyche. An excellent illustration of this is in Emily Bronte's novel *Wuthering Heights*, which has already been mentioned. The most striking figure in this tale is Heathcliff, who appears to be part man and part devil, and whose one driving goal in life is to unite with his beloved Cathy. However, Cathy, though she loves him deeply in her soul, resists him and betrays her truest feelings by marrying the innocuous and ineffective Edgar Linton. Heathcliff is not deterred, however, and

---

[23] Ibid., p. 129.
[24] Esther Harding, *The Way of All Women* (New York: David McKay Co., Inc., 1933, 1961), chap. 2.

persists in his efforts to unite with Cathy, even though this results in a conflict in her so great that, unwilling to bear it, she becomes ill and dies. The story then continues with Cathy's daughter, also named Cathy, as the heroine. The younger Cathy is persecuted relentlessly by the increasingly morose Heathcliff. However, unlike others who are destroyed under Heathcliff's persecution, the younger Cathy grows stronger. Eventually she marries Hareton, and as she works out her relationship with Hareton, Heathcliff withdraws more and more from the story until finally he unites in death with his Cathy. Thus at the end of the story there is a double marriage: the earthly pair, Catherine and Hareton, and the spirit couple, Heathcliff and Cathy.

In her brilliant analysis of the story, Barbara Hannah[25] points out that Heathcliff is a personification of the animus, and describes the way he functions in the psychology of a woman. He is a seemingly ruthless figure who destroys many people in the story, but he is not blind evil, for in the end he proves to be the very force that leads to psychological development. Because of him the weak are destroyed and only those who become strong survive, and it is through his persistent efforts that, in the end of the story, there is the double marriage that is a symbol of wholeness. Thus in Heathcliff we can see how the animus can appear to be demonic, yet in fact he contains in himself the mainspring for individuation and proves to be a relentless force that compels a woman to rid herself of weak, childish feelings and develop the true strength of her character. Heathcliff's relentless desire for union with Cathy is analogous to the relentless urge from within for the unification of a woman's personality, a process that the animus makes possible and even seems to insist on.

Jung first equated the animus with a woman's soul, just as he equated the anima with a man's soul. In "The Psychology of the Transference," he wrote, "It will be clear . . . that the 'soul' . . . has a feminine character in the man and a masculine character in the woman."[26] However, this identification of animus with soul has been disputed by many of Jung's women colleagues and disciples. For instance, Emma Jung, Barbara Hannah, and Irene

---

[25] Hannah, *Striving Towards Wholeness,* chap. 10.
[26] Jung, *CW* 16, p. 301.

de Castillejo all argue that the soul in woman is feminine just as it is in man, and that animus is not to be identified with soul, but with spirit. According to this way of thinking, the animus is not the soul, but leads a woman *to* her soul. It is for this reason that he has the value of a psychopomp, a guide, or one who points or leads the way.[27]

One helpful function the positive animus gives to a woman is the power of discrimination. Jung wrote that in feminine psychology "we are not dealing with a function of relationship (as with the anima) but, on the contrary, with a *discriminative* function, namely the animus."[28] Thus he virtually identified the animus with logos and the anima with eros, with, however, the misleading intimation that the animus was thereby identical with thinking in a woman, and the anima with feeling in a man. We have already seen that this is not the case—that a woman thinks for herself—it is not the animus who thinks for her—and that a man has his own feelings and his own capacity for love. Yet, in fact, Jung did not directly connect the animus with logos as such, much less with thinking, nor the anima with eros, but used these categories to give us conceptual approximations of the functions of these two realities. "The animus," he wrote, "corresponds to the paternal Logos just as the anima corresponds to the maternal Eros. But I do not wish or intend to give these two intuitive concepts too specific a definition. I use Eros and Logos merely as conceptual aids to describe the fact that woman's consciousness is characterized more by the connective quality of Eros than by the discrimination and cognition associated with Logos. In men, Eros, the function of relationship, is usually less developed than Logos. In women, on the other hand, Eros is an expression of their true nature."[29]

The animus can act like a guide who leads a woman to her soul because he uses his torch of discrimination and understanding to illuminate her inner world. He also acts as a bridge to the impersonal world of intellect and spirit, and gives her otherwise

---

[27] Cf. E. Jung, *Animus and Anima*; de Castillejo, *Knowing Woman*; Hannah, *Striving Towards Wholeness.*

[28] Jung, *CW* 16, p. 294.

[29] Jung, *CW* 9, 2, p. 14.

diffused consciousness a capacity for focused concentration. As is always the case when describing the anima and animus, images are more helpful than concepts, and Irene de Castillejo gives us a helpful image of the positive animus when she describes him as a "torchbearer." It is the animus, she says, who throws light on things, who enables a woman to focus her concentration, makes it possible for her to be objective, and opens up to her the world of knowledge for its own sake.

> To see clearly enough to know something quite definitely, so solidly that one can express it and say "This is my truth, here I take my stand," one needs the help of the animus himself.
>
> I personally like to think of my helpful animus as a torch-bearer; the figure of a man holding aloft his torch to light my way, throwing its beams into dark corners and penetrating the mists which shield the world of half-hidden mystery where, as a woman, I am so very much at home.
>
> In a woman's world of shadows and cosmic truths he makes a pool of light as a focus for her eyes, and as she looks she may say, "Ah yes, that's what I mean," or "Oh no, that's not my truth at all." It is with the help of this torch also that she learns to give form to her ideas. He throws light on the jumble of words hovering beneath the surface of her mind so that she can choose the ones she wants, separates light into the colours of the rainbow for her selection, enables her to see the part of which her whole is made, to discriminate between this and that. In a word, he enables her to focus.[30]

As a woman begins to relate to her inner self, de Castillejo continues, she first meets the animus, who, by throwing his torch into the interior and meanings of things, leads her into her inner recesses where her soul is to be found. But, she stresses, *he* is not her soul, for her soul is feminine like her ego. "As it is he whom a woman meets first he may appear to be himself the soul image she is seeking; but if she ventures with him further into the dark and unknown she may find that he does not represent her soul but is rather acting as her guide toward it."[31]

---

[30] De Castillejo, *Knowing Woman,* p. 76.
[31] Ibid., p. 166.

Thus the soul in a woman is feminine like herself, best described, perhaps, as a life force, a source of energy and love. For
a man, the soul is something other than himself, an elusive
though essential feminine reality that is indispensable to the well-
being of his consciousness. For a woman, the discovery of the
soul is the discovery of what is most essentially her own deepest,
truest nature. For a man, the world of objective knowledge and
impersonal goals comes naturally, while a woman needs, as it
were, to be initiated into a world to which she is not subjectively
related and which may come as a startling discovery.

So the animus is a thrower of light. But, de Castillejo warns
us, he *must* throw his light somewhere, and this means that the
woman must use the animus function in herself correctly and creatively. "It is the woman who is not using the animus creatively
who is at his mercy for he *must* throw his light somewhere. So he
attracts her attention by throwing his light on one formula or slo-
gan after another quite regardless of their exact relevance. She
falls into the trap and accepts what he shows her as gospel
truth."[32]

As with everything else in the psyche, the key word is relatedness. The animus is positive in his function when the woman is
correctly related to him, and negative when the relationship is in-
correct. The proper relationship with the animus is helped by
recognition of his reality, by giving him scope in life and main-
taining a dialogue with him just as if he were an inner husband.

To recognize the reality of the animus is to perceive the reality and autonomy of the unconscious. This always requires, as
we have seen, the recognition of projections when they occur; the
animus is particularly likely to project himself onto outer men
when he is not consciously perceived by a woman as a part of
herself. Such a projection can be perceived as having occurred
when a man is overvalued or undervalued, and especially when
he is seen to be fascinating. It can also be recognized by the reaction of the man himself because, unless he is so egocentric that he
feeds on such things, the man will react to a projection with in-
creasing discomfort, in the manner already described.

To give the animus reality and his proper place in life, a

---

[32] Ibid., p. 80.

woman must have a life that includes him. As we have seen with
the anima, the inner figures of the unconscious all want to live,
and they can do this only through our lives. A woman who ignores the objective side of life, and especially the development of
her intellectual and spiritual side, can expect to have a frustrated
animus who becomes troublesome and devilish as a consequence.
She often needs to have something in her life outside of the personal realm of family, husband, or lover. In this way she can sat-
isfy the animus. However, it should be noted that if a woman
goes too far in this matter she runs the danger of becoming too
identified with the animus. She may pursue masculine goals in
the world and develop the life of her intellect in academic and
professional pursuits only if she maintains an awareness of herself as a person with a feminine soul who also embodies a masculine principle.

Keeping a distinction between herself as woman and soul,
and the animus as masculine discriminatory power, is greatly aid-
ed by the process of dialogue, a process already mentioned as a
way in which a man can relate to his anima. The animus is often
first noticed by a woman as a "voice" within her, that is, as an
autonomous train of thoughts and ideas that flow into her consciousness. This autonomous stream of thoughts and ideas can be
personified as her inner man and a dialogue can be cultivated
with him. In this dialogue it is very helpful, Irene de Castillejo
points out, if a woman keeps the animus informed about how *she*
feels about things. The animus will be quite ready to intrude with
his opinions and ideas and plans, and can be ruthless in trying to
bring them about. The woman must be firm with him, and carefully instruct him in how she feels and what her needs and desires
are. In describing the case of one woman, Irene de Castillejo noted that the animus was "positive and helpful so long as the woman took the precaution of informing him how she, as woman, felt
about the matters in hand and only became negative when she
failed to do so. For then, being deprived of the essential data of
her feeling he had no alternative but to voice the general truths of
the day."[33]

Again and again in matters of the psyche we realize that

---

[33] Ibid., p. 168.

when we are correctly and consciously related to our inner figures they tend to assume their proper role and function, and when we are unaware of them, and do not have a correct relationship, they tend to possess us and disrupt our lives. So it is with the animus, who "is a woman's greatest friend when he shines his light on what is relevant, and turns foe the moment he lapses into irrelevance."[34]

---

[34] Ibid., p. 80.

Chapter Four

That mysterious life force which we call sexuality is both compli-
cated and enriched by the Invisible Partners. We have already
seen how the anima and animus are frequently projected onto
members of the opposite sex, and how, when a person carries for
us such a projected image, sexual feelings and fantasies are likely
to be aroused. This is because the archetypes of the anima and
animus are so numinous, that is, so charged with psychic energy that they grip us emotionally, and this energy usually affects
us first on the sexual level.

The kind of magnetic sexual attraction we may feel when the
anima or animus is projected in this manner leads to powerful
psychological ties with the person who is carrying that projection, in the manner we have described, and this phenomenon is
often disturbing to a long-term relationship such as marriage.
The projections of the anima and animus seldom remain on a
person, whose ordinary humanity becomes evident under the
stress and strain of daily life, and for this reason the projections
of the anima or animus will usually fall on persons outside of the
marriage relationship, which may prove to be a disturbing factor.

Numinosity, discovery, adventure, and curiosity usually enliven the initial relationship with members of the opposite sex,
but as they begin to wear off, sexual life between a man and wom-

an can become routine,[1] and sexual desires and fantasies may re-volve around other people. People who lack psychological under-standing may then suppose that they no longer love their mates, since they are now "in love" with someone else. Others, especial-ly those who have been raised in a strict religious tradition that has educated them to treat their fantasies as though they were, in themselves, sins, may be horrified at their fantasies and try to re-press them out of fear and guilt. Still others, who lack a certain moral stamina, may want to cast aside a marriage relationship that is being threatened with boredom, rather than to work on it, thinking that the new and fascinating relationship is now "it," and that if only they can possess the object of their sexual desires they will be happy.

As Adolf Guggenbuhl-Craig has pointed out,[2] this is partic-ularly likely to occur in our culture, where marriage is perceived in terms of what he calls "well-being" rather than "salvation." To view marriage in terms of well-being means that we marry with the thought that this will lead us to happiness, satisfaction, and a feeling of peace and plenitude. To view marriage in terms of salvation means that we see marriage as one possible path to self-knowledge and individuation. In marriage two people bump up against each other's areas of unconsciousness. This affords both people an opportunity to become aware of personal qualities or habits that they see only when their partners in the experience of daily living object to them.

Such a relationship provides an excellent container in which individuation can occur, for people who can work through areas

---

[1] Fortunately for sexual life in marriage, there are certain advantages to the married or permanent relationship when it comes to sexual fulfillment. In a per-manent relationship, for instance, a couple has an opportunity to learn about each other as sexual partners, to discover what pleases each other, and to be-come adept at being a lover well-suited for his or her partner. It is also impor-tant that in a long-term relationship the factor of personal love and relatedness may more than make up for the fact that the projected image of the anima and animus no longer surrounds one's partner. If, in addition, a married couple can keep their fantasies alive in their sexual life, perhaps sharing them with each other and expressing them in their love life, sexuality in marriage can remain a vital part of the relationship.

[2] Adolf Guggenbuhl-Craig, *Marriage—Dead or Alive*, trans. Murray Stein (Zurich: Spring Publications, 1977), pp. 36ff.

of unconsciousness in their life together can mature in their capacity to love and relate to another human being. If we value marriage only when it offers us a sense of well-being, we will not have the intestinal fortitude to work through these painful experiences, but if we learn to value marriage because of the opportunities it offers for salvation—that is, individuation—as well as for its other blessings, our marriage relationship is on a more solid footing.

However, the question will remain: How are we to regard fantasies about another person outside of our marriage that may be inspired by the projections we have discussed? It is clear that it can be destructive to be pulled into such fantasies without any conscious regard for their underlying meaning. But it can be equally unfortunate if an overly developed conscience causes a person to reject his or her anima- or animus-inspired fantasies, for such fantasies contain a great deal of important psychic energy. For this reason it is often better to try to understand the meaning of our fantasies than to reject them out of hand because of their supposed devilishness, for there is nothing wrong with having fantasies as such. Fantasies simply come uninvited into our minds for reasons of their own; it is what we do with our fantasies that is a matter of morality.

If our erotic thoughts have been directed to another person by the anima or animus, there may be many messages for us. When this happens, perhaps the first thing to examine is the quality of our primary relationship. For instance, many men have a passive eros, that is, they are not active in establishing close ties with women, they tend to look on women as mothers and providers and not as companions and lovers. Consequently they remain undeveloped on the side of feeling and relationship. When this happens, the anima may attempt to stir them up by creating all kinds of fantasies in their minds. It is as though the anima recognizes the inadequacy and sleepiness of the man in the area of personal relationships and love, and decides to stir up the pot. Or, it may be that a man or a woman is married to the wrong person, has been unwilling or unable to face this fact, but is led to examine his or her primary relationship more honestly by the intrusion into consciousness of anima- or animus-inspired fantasies about other people.

For instance, a man came to therapy because he had been impotent with his wife for many years. He also was troubled because of his erotic fantasies for another woman. After he had talked for a few hours it became clear to him that he simply did not *like* his wife. It was not a matter of loving or not loving her, he did not *like* her, and really did not want to be with her. It was the first time he had allowed himself to face this fact. Once he faced this honestly, he sought out the other woman and immediately his impotence vanished. It was as though his penis did not lie; it was telling him all along that he simply did not want the woman to whom he was married. Of course this man had to go through all kinds of hell in separating from his wife, and he had to carry a certain burden of guilt, for, as could be expected, his wife felt unwanted and rejected. There are no simple solutions to love problems in life, and every love relationship requires a price from us.

The chances are, however, that the appearance of the anima or animus in a projected form is simply an effort on the part of these inner figures to gain our attention, in the manner already noted. An attempt must then be made to withdraw the projection, that is, to understand that the attraction or fascination we feel for another person stems from the projected psychic content within us. In this way we can begin to relate to the numinous image of the anima or animus as an inner factor of our own psyche, and thus begin to achieve that vital relationship with the unconscious which is such an aid in our process of individuation. Of course, as was noted in chapter one, projections can never be withdrawn completely, for they are out of our conscious control; nor can we ever become so conscious of the inner images of the anima and animus that projections do not occur. Withdrawing projections does not mean that they no longer occur, but that we understand them as images within ourselves when they do.

A special instance of anima projection in masculine psychology comes from the problem of the "double anima." The anima often comes up in a man's psychology as a double figure. The first anima image may draw a man to wife, family, and home. The second anima image draws a man into a world of emotionally toned experiences or images outside of the wife-children-home pattern. (We can call one image endogamous and the other exogamous.) Many men initially fulfil the first anima image and proceed to settle down to the pleasures and satisfactions of family life, only to find that their consciousness is later stirred by the second anima image, for the effect of the anima is always to "stir up" a man's consciousness to greater life. It is as though the second image comes in order to awaken a man to further inner development, or lead him into more life experiences. She serves to keep his eros from becoming too passive, his state of mind from being too satisfied, comfortable, and, eventually, stagnant. In short, she brings fire into a man's life, and adds color to his personality.

When such anima entanglements develop in a man there are no rules about how to proceed. Theology may try to lay down general principles for the regulation of mankind's love life, but psychology cannot do this, for matters of eros permit only individual solutions. Each man must find his own way through the labyrinth of relationships, emotions, yearnings, and complications that the emergence of the double anima image always brings.

There may be some men who need concrete experiences with women in order to realize their own emotions and begin to understand what women mean to them. This may particularly be true for a man who has not had sufficient experience in matters of women, love, and relationship; who has, as it were, an "unlived life" in this area.

A man who is "caught" by the anima, and drawn by her toward a relationship with another woman, will have to take into account his primary relationship. Many men, out of loyalty and love for their wives, quite correctly (for them) refuse to have a relationship with another woman. Some men, however, do have such a relationship, but keep it a secret, telling themselves that they do not want to hurt their wives, and that what their partners do not know will not hurt them. Usually the truth is that they do not want to go through the emotional difficulties of telling their wives the dilemma they are in and what they are doing. Most men do not like unpleasant emotional scenes and, understandably enough, their wives are likely to be hurt, angry, and perhaps vindictive if they know that their husbands are sharing their love with other women. "What my wife (or husband) doesn't know won't hurt her (or him)" usually translates, "I don't have the courage to go through the emotional hassle of bringing things out into the open."

If an extramarital relationship is frequent or long-lasting, the spouse is certain to be affected by it eventually via the unconscious, that is, there will be effects on the psyche of the marriage partner even if on a conscious level that person does not know that anything is going on. Occasionally it happens, for instance, that a person comes to analysis because of a marriage relationship that is disturbed, yet he or she is unable to pinpoint the problem. When discussion with the spouse is attempted, nothing comes from it. Later it usually comes out that one of them has been involved in a relationship with someone else for some time. Then it is clear why the marriage partner acted so differently at different times, why so often there was a kind of secretiveness, and why their discussions seemed to bear little fruit. There are even cases in which a person dreamt that his or her partner was involved with someone else. Naturally the dreamer was disturbed by this, but did not know what to do with the dream because the facts were not known.

So in the long run the extramarital affair that is kept secret is usually unfair to the other person in the marriage, and, when it comes to light, it is found that damage has been caused by the secrecy. The one who has been unaware of the partner's involvement feels hurt and slighted, and, of course, the trust between the two people has been injured and may be difficult to rebuild. Also, a person who loves secretly tends to damage himself or herself. For one thing, it takes energy to keep a secret. Secrets are like corks that can be held under water only by applying constant pressure. For this reason we lose some psychic energy when we keep a secret life hidden. A man also damages his own soul when he damages the woman in his life because he alienates the anima. We cannot try to find happiness and fulfillment at someone else's expense without damaging our own souls in the process. In more metaphysical language, an attempt to find happiness at the expense of others develops a bad "karma" within us, that is, it causes retribution from within.

And what of the anima who is behind all of these complications, whose projected image onto the other woman has entangled a man in fantasies, aroused his yearnings, and stirred up his unfulfilled emotional life? It often seems as though she does not care about the difficulties she is creating. Like Aphrodite, her concern is that men and women love and make love, and she is not concerned with human happiness. So there is this difficulty for a man: Human relationships, which call for an ethical and moral attitude, and for their continued success require qualities of integrity and fair play, are greatly troubled by an anima who doesn't care about these matters as long as she succeeds in stirring up more life. Yet it is not true that Aphrodite has no morality, for her moral code extends to all matters of relationship. In the long run, if a man is faithless in matters of love and relationship, the goddess within turns on him with a vengeance and demands retribution in the form of what has been called "feminine justice."

As Marie-Louise von Franz has pointed out,[3] there is feminine justice as well as masculine justice. Masculine justice is impersonal and objective. It is enshrined in our legal code and penal system, and calls for an impartial and uniform meting out of justice as society requires it, for various offenses, without regard to individual considerations. Feminine justice, on the other hand, is the justice of nature. It is personal, and suited to the particular circumstances.

An example of feminine justice is the story of a woman who advertised a new-model Porsche for sale at the ridiculously low price of $75.00.[4] A man read the ad and contacted the woman. "I have only a check," he is reported to have told her. "That will be perfectly all right," the woman said. Amazed and delighted at his good fortune, the man gave her the check and drove off in the Porsche, but his conscience troubled him and he returned to her and said, "Lady, do you know what this car is worth?" "Oh yes," she answered. "Well then why are you selling it to me for only $75.00?" "Well," she replied, "It is like this. My husband left yesterday for Europe with his mistress and said to me, 'Sell the

---

[3] Von Franz, *Feminine in Fairy Tales*, pp. 33–34.

[4] This story was reported to me by people who heard it over the radio and read it in the newspaper. The quotations may not be exact. Factual or not, it illustrates what feminine justice means.

Porsche for me and send me the check.' " Now *that* is feminine justice. The essence of it? Her husband got *just what he deserved.*

Feminine justice prevails in matters of human relationship, and also in the matter of our relationship with the unconscious and with nature. If we alienate the unconscious, or damage or ignore the laws and demands of Mother Nature, we get what we deserve. That is, there is a punishment meted out that exactly fits the individual circumstances. Thus if we abuse our bodies, we pay the appropriate price; when we contaminate the air and earth and sea, nature metes out a punishment to us, as we are just beginning to realize. When we despise the unconscious, justice will be demanded from within us by all those inner powers whom we have offended, and if we are false in our relationships, we have to pay a price of some kind.

I have discussed the problem of a man's double anima image, but a woman also has a double animus image, as Robert Johnson has shown in his study of the Hindu story "The Transposed Heads."[5] When the animus comes up as a double image, one man may carry part of her animus for a woman, and another man may carry another part. Because these animus images are projected, the woman finds herself torn between the two men, for she experiences a different part of herself coming into being as she comes into relationship with each man. Naturally she has great difficulty in making a choice between the two men, for until she is able to take back the parts of her psyche that have been projected she is compulsively related to both of them, and finds it as difficult to give up one of them as she would find it difficult to give up her right or left arm. Her difficulty may be resolved, however, as she withdraws the projections through becoming conscious of them, and also as the personal relationship, as differentiated from the relationship that is engendered through projection, begins to develop more intensely with one man than with the other.

It is quite natural for a young woman to first experience her own personality through relationships with different men. One

---

[5] From a lecture by this title given by Robert Johnson in 1979 for the Friends of Jung. Available from the Friends of Jung Tape Library, P.O. Box 33114, San Diego, Calif. 92103.

young woman was sent to me by her parents for counseling because she went so quickly from one unlikely love affair to another. And it was true that she had a bewildering number of different men in her life: students, sailors, older men, young men, white men, black men—there seemed to be no rhyme or reason to it. It was as though a different facet of her personality emerged with each relationship. Eventually, however, she did make a choice, married one of the men, and lived a monogamous life. It was important for this young woman to go through this phase of her development. In some cases, when a woman marries quite young, the need for such experiences may not have been met. If romantic fantasies have not been properly lived out in youth, and if there are elements of emotional immaturity, and unlived life may emerge into consciousness later and disturb the marriage.

Many people feel that monogamy is more natural to women than it is to men. This may be, but it may also be that women, in general, are more personally related than men. That is, a woman who has decided on who "her man" is, is less likely to be diverted to other relationships by her fantasies than is a man whose capacity for personal relationship is not as well developed. Of course this is a generalization and sometimes it may be the man who has more capacity for personal relationship than the woman and who is, accordingly, more resistant to seductive fantasies about other people.

However, where a woman's energy is drawn toward personal relationships, and especially toward developing a family, her monogamous tendencies may prevail. Once such a woman has emotionally accepted a man as her partner, she tends to exclude other men from her emotional life, just as the ovum, once it has acepted one sperm, shuts the other sperms out. In our present time the monogamous tendency among women does not appear to be as great as it was previously—at least many women report today that they can have more than one man in their lives at the same time. Men have often been said to be more polygamous by nature, and, in our culture, may have to sacrifice some of this tendency in order to make a monogamous marriage work, but this too is a generalization and there are certainly many men whose emotional lives center around one, and only one, woman.

Whether it be a man or a woman, the most important thing

to remember when the anima or animus stirs up our erotic thoughts is that the underlying force behind them is the drive of the unconscious to relate to consciousness. The union of the personality is represented in the imagery of the unconscious as a great love affair. The opposites within us are so far apart that only the great unifying power of eros can bring them together. This can be said to be the common denominator, the basic psychological fact, in all love affairs, and for the person who wishes to become whole it is the great underlying factor that can never be disregarded.

It is clear from what has been said that sexual fantasies and yearnings are closely connected with inner psychological processes. A word about the symbolic meaning of such fantasies is in order at this point.

As a rule of thumb, it can be said that what we yearn for sexually is a symbolic representation of what we need in order to become whole. This means that sexual fantasies symbolically complement ego consciousness in a way that points us toward wholeness. Understanding the symbolic meaning of our sexual fantasies enables us to become less compulsive regarding them, that is, instead of being driven and possessed by them, our range of consciousness can be expanded by them.

The most frequent example of how a sexual yearning represents what is needed to bring us to wholeness is the sexual desire of a man for a woman, and of a woman for a man. Images of a woman appear in a man's sexual fantasies because she represents his missing half, the other side of his personality to which he needs to relate if he is to be complete, and vice versa with a woman. Of course this is not to say that this is *all* that sexual yearnings mean. There is always the desire for physical release of tension, for the meeting of body with body, and for the closeness and intimacy with another person that sexuality achieves and expresses. But it is to say that in addition to these aspects of sexuality there is also a spiritual or psychological meaning.

Sexual fantasies are usually complex. We do not simply yearn for a woman or for a man, but have fantasies about the object of our desire in a particular way. There may be all kinds of romantic stories that accompany our desires, or there may be fantasies of seduction or rape. The possibilities of sexual fantasies are innumerable, and it is quite natural for people to have highly colorful sexual fantasies. If the content of these fantasies becomes too unusual, we call them "perversions," but it is too bad if this leads us to dismiss them out of hand; instead we need to understand why we have this particular sexual fantasy, that is, what the fantasy symbolically expresses.

Edward C. Whitmont, in his book *The Symbolic Quest*,[6] gives us an example of how one man's unusual sexual fantasy represented symbolically exactly what changes he needed to undergo in order to become more whole. Whitmont's client came to him because he was incapable of having sexual intercourse with a woman until he had first kissed her feet. Naturally, this sexual fantasy was disturbing to him and he saw himself as perverted in some way. Analysis revealed that this man was unusually identified with his intellect and regarded himself as superior to women; accordingly he devalued the feminine side of himself and of life and cultivated an arrogant masculinity. In the act of kissing a woman's foot he had, symbolically, to lower his head. His sexual fantasies and desires thus forced the man to do symbolically what he had to accomplish psychologically in order to become a more whole person: sacrifice the domination of his intellect, give up his masculine arrogance, and, as it were, worship what he had hitherto devalued. As long as he did not understand the meaning of his sexual fantasies, Whitmont's client was simply seized by them compulsively and driven to act them out. As he began to understand what his fantasies meant, and why he had them, he was led to a change of consciousness, and became both more free in his love making and more whole as a person. One could say that his sexual fantasy came to cure him of a maladaptation of consciousness. The sexual fantasy was not an illness; he was one-sided and out of balance in his development and the sexual fantasy was produced by the unconscious to correct this.

Adolf Guggenbuhl-Craig gives us another example.[7] A student whom he once had as a client had gotten into trouble with

[6] Edward C. Whitmont, *The Symbolic Quest*, (Princeton, N.J.: Princeton University Press, 1978 edition), pp. 20–23.

[7] Guggenbuhl-Craig, *Marriage*, p. 84.

the police because of a sexual compulsion to steal female under-
wear. One day, Guggenbuhl-Craig reports, his client came in to
him triumphantly and read to him a passage from Goethe's poem
Faust in which Faust meets the beautiful Helen: Faust, after a
long search, finally meets this most beautiful feminine being in
the world, only to have her disappear, leaving Faust standing
there with her garment and veil in his hands. The young man
concluded from this story that he was seized by a vision of the
beauty of the eternal feminine image, which was symbolized by
the feminine garment that so occupied his sexual thoughts. The
object of his desire, in short, was not woman as such but what
woman symbolized to him: the eternal feminine with all of her
majesty and numinosity. Like Faust, he had glimpsed somewhere
a vision of this, but had been left with only the symbol of the garment in his hands.

Another common sexual fantasy among men as they enter
into middle age is the fantasy of meeting and relating sexually
with a much younger woman. In many respects, of course, the
meaning of such fantasies is obvious, since younger women may
be supposed to be more physically attractive. But on a deeper level
these desires express the difficulty a man encounters in accepting
the fact that he is aging, his desire to hang on to life and retard
the progress of the years, and, at its deepest level, his hunger for
the renewal of his consciousness and for immortal life. The latter
desires cannot be fulfilled through any sexual relationship, of
course, but can be fulfilled through a contact with the unconscious that the anima provides, that is, through individuation.
Such a fantasy thus expresses not so much a physical desire as a
religious need.

Fantasies such as these are quite impersonal; they operate
within us independently of any personal or feeling relationship to
any particular individual. They are a kind of impersonal sexuality
that might or might not be conjoined with personal love and feeling for a sexual partner. Men in particular seem prone to discon-
nect their sexual lives from their personal feelings, while women
are more likely to report that they cannot do this, that their sexual feelings, while every bit as intense if not more intense than
a man's, are more romantic and more personally oriented to a
particular person to whom they feel close.

It is because there is so much symbolic meaning in sexual fantasies that Adolf Guggenbuhl-Craig has referred to them as "individuation fantasies." In his book he says, "Sexuality, with all its variations, can be understood as an individuation fantasy, a fantasy whose symbols are so alive and so effective that they even influence our physiology . . . sexual life, above all as it shows itself in fantasy, is an intensive individuation process in symbols. This form of the process must be respected and recognized." He goes on to argue that sexual fantasies that seem to deviate from the "norm" should not be pathologized. "The sexual fantasies of most men and women are wilder and more bizarre than actual sexual life as it is lived. Unfortunately, analysts and psychologists often react to such fantasies condescendingly and pathologize them. A commentary on a particularly lively and unusual sexual fantasy of a patient might be the following: 'This young man—or woman—is not yet capable of relationship. He is still completely the victim of his non-human sexual instinct.' "[8] This disparaging attitude on the part of therapists toward sexual fantasies simply engenders guilt, inhibitions, and isolation, and prevents a patient from more openly investigating important psychological processes. This negative attitude came partly, at least, from Freud, who regarded all sexual desires except the most "normal" as symptoms of maldevelopment. Currently therapists are changing to a much more accepting attitude that regards a variety of sexual fantasies as natural and tries to reduce guilt about them, though the living out of sexual fantasies is another matter, of course. However, there is very little understanding among therapists today of the symbolic meaning of such fantasies, even among those who are more progressively oriented than the old-style psychiatrists.

What to do with the sexual energy aroused by our fantasies is, of course, a difficult question. When, where, and how sexual life should be lived out has always been a moral and social problem of great complexity, and different cultures have had different attitudes toward it.

Christian culture has generally been exceedingly restrictive of the sexual impulse, as will be seen in more detail later. Because

---

[8] Ibid., pp. 82–83.

of this a peculiar situation has existed in our culture: We tend to impart to children the feeling that sexuality is bad, yet at the same time we give young people every opportunity to experiment with this fascinating instinct. Every psychotherapist hears stories from his or her clients of childhood sexual experiences that were shrouded in secrecy and guilt, which the child kept hidden from parents out of fear of punishment or a vague but powerful feeling of having done something wrong. The result is that a lot of guilt tends to become associated with sex, which damages the instinctual life. In contrast, American Indian culture reversed this. In Indian culture, sexuality was regarded as something natural and innocent, but at the same time young people were carefully watched to make sure that it was not expressed until the proper time had come for it. No doubt much psychological damage was avoided in this way. At the present time in our culture the picture is changing. Christian restrictiveness is giving way to license; where before there were too many restrictions, now there are sometimes none at all. It might be said that constipation has given way to diarrhea, but the one has never been known to be the cure for the other. Too much direct expression of sexual life, without regard for the elements of romance, personal relationship, and psychological understanding of its meaning, damages the spiritual life just as too many restrictions damage the instinctual life. The two, of course, affect each other. A person whose instinctual life is damaged suffers sooner or later from atrophy of the spiritual life as well, and damage to the spiritual life sooner or later results in a jaded instinctual life that has lost its dynamism. In fact, sometimes men become impotent when they are continuing to live out an unbridled sexuality after the time has come for them to sacrifice some of their sexual desires for the sake of a different level of consciousness. For the sensual and the spiritual are not separate realities; both embody the same mystery. The life of the spirit may well be enhanced by the physical expression of sexuality; many people need to find and express the fire of the spirit through sensuality and other physical expressions of their bodies, such as dancing. On the other hand, sexual tension and the quality of sexual life can be increased by allying the physical instinct with a developing spiritual consciousness.

If sexual fantasies become compulsive, or if living them out

concretely would be destructive to our important personal relationships, we may need to make special efforts to bring the energy of such fantasies to a higher level of consciousness in a special
way. This is where we need psychology to help us understand
their symbolic meaning. Active imagination, in the manner described in the appendix to this book, may also be particularly
helpful in this task.

A special instance of sexual fantasy life lies in the area of
male homosexuality,[9] and because homosexuality is so frequent
among men these fantasies are worth some special comments.

To begin with, to refer to homosexuality as though it is a
uniform phenomenon is misleading, for there are many expressions of male sexuality that we call homosexual that actually dif-
fer markedly. In general, we refer to homosexuality whenever a
man has a sexual erotic desire for another male, or for the male
organ. Yet such desires may take quite varied forms. Some men
are exclusively homosexual and have intimate relationships only
with other men. But others marry, have children, and develop a
satisfactory heterosexual life, yet are overwhelmed from time to
time with what appears to be a desire for a homosexual experience.

In the latter case, we often find that a middle-aged or older
man has fallen in love with a younger man who has the attributes
of a young Adonis. The young man who receives the love of the
older man seems to embody in himself both masculine and feminine virtues. Typically he has a strong, virile body, yet he also
has certain feminine attributes and graces that give him a beautiful, youthful quality; he appears as a young David, an Antinous,[10]
or a young god, rather than as a one-sidedly masculine person.
Such a youth receives the projection of the Self, the image of
wholeness in the psyche of the older man. Most men, as we have
seen, project their missing half, the feminine element, onto a

---

[9] I am going to confine my remarks to male homosexuality, for I do not feel
I have sufficient knowledge to venture into the subject of homosexuality among
women.

[10] The young lover of the Roman Emperor Hadrian. See Marguerite Your-
cenar, *Memoirs of Hadrian* (New York: Farrar, Strauss and Co., 1963).

woman. The man then represents the masculine side, and the woman the feminine side, of a masculine-feminine totality. In the instance we are now considering, however, totality is represented in the young man, who seems to include both masculine and feminine in himself. The actual young man is himself not this complete person; he is simply the carrier of the projection of the androgynous soul of the older man. In fact, when the two people get to know each other as human beings, they may be keenly disappointed in each other.

So there are some men whose other side, which represents wholeness for them, is not represented by a woman, but by this figure of the androgynous, divine youth. Marie-Louise von Franz writes, "There is the same idea in Persian teaching which says that after death the noble man meets either a youth who looks exactly like himself, . . . or a girl of fifteen, . . . and if he asks the figure who it is, then it will say, 'I am thy own self.' "[11]

A good example of this kind of homoerotic desire is found in Thomas Mann's novelette *Death in Venice*. Author Mann says of the aging Aschenbach, who has fallen in love with the youthful Tadzio, "His eyes took in the proud bearing of that figure there at the blue water's edge; with an outburst of rapture he told himself that what he saw was beauty's very essence; form as divine thought, the single and pure perfection which resides in the mind, of which an image and likeness, rare and holy, was here raised up for adoration."[12]

Such a projection of the Self onto a younger man is possible because the Self image is typically represented for a man as either an older man or a younger man, as Marie-Louise von Franz has pointed out in her book *The Feminine in Fairy Tales*.[13] This helps us understand the strong bond that sometimes springs up between a young man and an older man. For the young man, the Self is carried by the older man, who represents the positive fa-

---

[11] Marie-Louise von Franz, *Puer Aeternus* (Zurich: Spring Publications, 1970), p. IX–17.

[12] Thomas Mann, *Death in Venice* (New York: Random House, 1936), p. 44.

[13] Pp. 151–152. For a woman, an older or a younger woman might carry the projection of the Self image.

ther, power, and the authority of the Self. For the older man, the Self is carried by the youth, who represents son, eros, and the eternally youthful aspect of the Self. Because these projections are so numinous, and the longing for a relationship with the Self is so great, the bond between them readily becomes tinged with sexuality, and becomes what we think of as a homosexual relationship. Indeed, the relationship does tend to become sexual, but at its core there is the longing for wholeness, and energy for the relationship is supplied by the deep need each of the men has to integrate into himself what the other represents.

As we have seen, we tend to long sexually for whatever it is that we lack in our conscious development. In the case of the older man who longs for the young man, we usually find a person who has been too connected to the senex archetype, that is, too rigid, too aging, too caught up in the drive for power, or too intellectual. So the longing is for eros, for the puer or eternal youth, in short, for the spirit, in the form of a symbolic figure that compensates the man's conscious one-sidedness and offers to bring the ecstasy of totality.

In other types of homosexuality the object of sexual desire may not be another male as such, but a yearning for contact with the male organ. Again, this may occur in a man who is married, or has an otherwise normal heterosexual life, into which this homoerotic yearning intrudes from time to time. Often such a yearning represents symbolically a deep need for connection with the Self, represented by the phallus, symbol of the creative masculine spirit. Such a longing often intrudes into a man's consciousness when he feels particularly exhausted or fragmented, and needs the healing and synthesizing of his ego through a contact with the Self. It may also come as a compensation for too much exposure to the woman, both the woman within and the woman without, for man finds woman dangerous, and in order to maintain himself in relationship to her he must from time to time renew and consolidate his masculinity.

It is quite common to find among all of these men we have described a love problem of long standing. Often there was too little love between the mother and the boy, or the wrong kind of possessive or overwhelming love. Of equal importance, however, may be the missing love of the father. There is a time in a boy's life when he needs and craves love from his father, including physical expressions of the father's affection for him. In the type of homoerotic yearning we have described there usually has been a lack of such expressions of love between the boy and his father. Either the father was missing, or was not capable of that kind of love, or hated and rejected the boy, or was such a weak man that his love was not worth having. Such unfulfilled needs in the area of masculine affection create an uncertainty in the developing ego of the boy about his own masculinity, for masculine identification in a boy develops partly as a result of the boy's identification with his father and the resulting feeling that he is included in the world of men as a man among men.

This need will be particularly great if the mother's animus is directed toward the boy in a way that cuts him off from his budding, primitive masculine side. As von Franz has pointed out,[14] in an effort to socialize the boy a woman may allow her animus to cut him off from too much of his budding masculinity, the kind of boyish masculinity that tracks dirt into the house, uses dirty words, and struts about like a bantam rooster. Such outbreaks of boyish earthiness are, naturally, difficult for the mother to accept on a social level, yet they contain the seeds of a later positive masculine development. Too often the mother's animus squashes these signs of masculinity in the boy too much, and, especially in a sensitive youngster, the boy may lose touch with that side of himself as a result. An overly strict religious training may reinforce this process, stressing too much the values of kindness, forgiveness, and so forth, when the boy has not yet succeeded in first becoming confident of his budding masculine prowess.

When this happens, the young man's unfulfilled needs for primitive masculine development, and for the masculine affection he missed from his father, may be reflected in sexualized yearnings for closeness with other males. Women, on the other hand, are shunned, for a man has a fear of the sexual power of woman, her emotionality and her animus, which can be assuaged only

---

[14] Marie-Louise von Franz, *A Psychological Interpretation of The Golden Ass of Apuleius* (Zurich: Spring Publications, 1970), pp. XIII–10ff. and II–3ff. Cf. *Puer Aeternus.*

when a man is sufficiently confident of his chthonic, instinctual masculine side.

This is why at puberty young men in primitive cultures are initiated by the men into an exclusively masculine world via trials of strength and secret rites. Women are prohibited from witnessing these male rites, not only, perhaps, because they might prove a softening influence, but also because they might laugh, and this would wound the masculine self-esteem that the boy so greatly needs to build up. In addition to the trials of strength and the endurance of pain that these rites contain, which serve to strengthen the boy's ego, there is the transmission to the young man of the spiritual lore of the tribe that is passed down from the older men to the younger. Thus the boy comes into the possession of secrets known only to the men (an analogous lore is passed down from the older women to the young women in female initiation). Only after the boy is properly initiated into this all-masculine world is he ready for contact with the fascinating but dangerous world of women. Our present culture makes no provision for this kind of initiation ritual, and a good deal of what we call homosexuality is an attempt to fill the psychological need that is left by this omission.

We have been considering types of homosexuality that seem to represent an incompleted masculine development, or the projection of the soul image in an androgynous form. However, there are other types of homosexuality where the anima seems to play the dominant role because she seems to be in more or less complete control of the man's ego. In these cases, the qualities of the anima have, as it were, homogenized themselves with the masculine ego qualities and produced a kind of feminized male ego. This leads to what we might call classic homosexuality. While usually a man identifies his ego with masculinity, or tries to, this type of man has refused or has been unable to make such a masculine identification, and his ego structure has a certain hermaphroditic structure as a result. In his ego psychology, consequently, the anima plays a dominant role. Under such conditions heterosexual relationships are out of the question, for the opposites cannot relate and unite until they have first been separated and distinguished from each other. Homosexual relationships, therefore, are the norm for such a man.

These men may have many positive qualities. They can be quite sensitive, are often easy to talk with, frequently have a gentle, healing quality, and are given to artistic inclinations. In primitive communities, many shamans were homosexual, and in our own day there are certain individuals with healing gifts who have such a homosexual disposition. On the negative side, they can be peevish, fickle in relationships, and oversensitive, which often makes long-lasting, intimate relationships difficult.

The American Indians had an explanation for this kind of homosexuality that is as good as any I know, even though it is couched in mythological rather than scientific terms. The Indians believed that during puberty the moon appeared to a boy offering him a bow and arrow in one hand, and a woman's pack strap in the other. If the boy hesitated when reaching for the bow and arrow, then the moon handed him the pack strap. These young men became "berdaches," or homosexuals. They wore a special kind of dress and performed special functions in the tribe. For instance, they often served as matchmakers, and while they did not go to war, as did the other young men, they might accompany the war party to care for the wounded. Berdaches were perfectly accepted in the Indian community. They were not ridiculed or despised, but simply regarded as a special sort of man.[15] In psychological language, this is a way of saying that if a young man does not reach out to identify himself with his masculinity, symbolized by the bow and arrow, he falls into the hands of the anima.

There are few more convincing demonstrations of the reality of the anima in a man than these types of masculine homosexuality in which the presence of the feminine power is so conspicuous. In mannerisms, dress, the language system that arises in the subculture such men create for themselves, even in assumed feminine names, these men show forth the reality of the anima to an otherwise unbelieving world. It may be that a certain number of males in each generation are chosen in some way by the unconscious to live life in such a hermaphroditic way, that they are fated, as Jung once said,[16] to refuse to identify with "the role of a

---

[15] Cf. *Indians* (Alexandria, Va.: Time-Life Books, 1973), p. 129.
[16] Jung, *CW* 9, 1, p. 71.

one-sided sexual being," as though to remind us that no one is exclusively male or female, but that each of us has an androgynous nature.

In addition to men with a homoerotic tendency or homosexual nature there are other, heterosexual men who also lie very close to the feminine archetype. These men have succeeded in making a male ego identification, and their sexual feelings and love needs are directed toward women, but it is as though the feminine archetype is unusually numinous to them and looms large in their psychology. They too are often sensitive men with healing gifts or artistic inclinations, although their proximity to the anima may result in unusual sexual fantasies. These fantasies, as Guggenbuhl-Craig has pointed out,[17] should not be regarded as perverse, for they may be evidence of a potentially sensitive and differentiated personality. With these men, the Dr. Zhivagos of our society, there seems to be a need to be initiated into the meaning and mystery of the feminine on all of its levels. Such men are called on to understand women, to understand the feminine in themselves, to recognize and give importance to feminine values in life, and to have an immediate and personal experience with the unconscious. In this way they become initiates, as it were, of the Great Goddess. Such an initiation into the meaning of the feminine does not feminize these men, for in understanding the feminine they also differentiate the feminine from themselves. Their ego remains masculine, but is transformed by this initiation into a more differentiated state of consciousness. These cases suggest that the psychological influence of the anima is greater in some men than in others. Because of her numinosity, the anima exerts a profound influence on the psychology of certain men, fating them to lead a special kind of life that requires them to acquire unusual self-knowledge.

It is this numinous element that the anima introduces that can enter into sexuality and be the link between sexuality and religion. If we used the language of ancient times we would say that a god or goddess has entered into the situation whenever sexual attraction becomes numinous. In psychological language we would say that an archetype is exerting its fascination on us.

---

[17] *Marriage*, p. 78.

Thus in sexuality we not only seek the satisfaction of physical needs, the release of physical tensions, and, sometimes, psychological intimacy with other people; we can also be expressing our longing for ecstasy, that is, for an enlargement of narrow ego consciousness through contact with the divine. If, however, our consciousness is at a low level, the religious urges contained in sexuality are not fulfilled. At its worst, we then have only expressions of greed and egocentric desires and not the fulfillment of our need for ecstasy. For the religious side of sexuality to be fulfilled, we must relate to the archetypal factors in sexual desires in the correct way. We need to "worship" them by giving them correct and conscious attention.

The connection between sexuality and religion leads Adolf Guggenbuhl-Craig to make the interesting observation that while Freud tried to show that religion was a sublimation of sexuality, it is closer to the truth to say that sexuality can be, at its heart, the expression of mankind's religious urge, that is, the urge to ecstasy and wholeness. He writes,

> Freud sought in his own very impressive way to understand all of the so-called higher activities of man (such as art, religion, etc.) as sublimated sexuality. We can attempt to turn this around and to ask: can the totality of sexuality be comprehended from the viewpoint of individuation, of the religious impulse? Are the deeply sexually-colored love songs of medieval nuns really, as Freud would have it, expressions of frustrated eroticism? Do the many modern songs and the folk-songs that sing sentimentally about love and leave-taking have to do only with the unlived sexuality of adolescence? Or are they symbolic forms of expression for individuation processes and for the religious quest?[18]

So far in discussing sexuality and sexual fantasies very little has been said about love. I have discussed being in love, but not love in the sense of personal caring between one person and another. Later I will make a few comments about love, but the fact of the matter is that love is a great mystery that is not understood. We can describe psychologically what happens when we are "in love," and to a certain extent can understand this powerful phe-

---

[18] Ibid., p. 80.

nomenon, and we can discuss sexuality in its objective, impersonal workings. But why one human being should truly love another, why we are capable of actually caring for another person to the point where we are willing and able to sacrifice for that person is a sublime mystery. If I have not discussed love at more length it is not because it is unimportant, but because it is *so* important that to psychologize it or make pronouncements about it is to *de*value it, not value it. When all is said and done, after all the discussion of being in love, sexuality, fantasies, projections, and so forth, we wind up confronted by something we know practically nothing about: human love.

Another reason that the nature of love is so hard to discuss in a book such as this is because of its highly individual quality. Inevitably in this discussion I have had to make generalizations, but the expression of eros is, in the last analysis, always an individual matter. As von Franz once pointed out, no love problem can be solved by following a general principle. "If there is a solution," she wrote, "it can only be unique, from individual to individual, from one woman to one man. Eros is in its essence only meaningful if it is completely, uniquely individual."[19] For this reason, while I feel able to make certain general statements about projection, transference, sexuality, and so forth, it is impossible to make general statements about the mystery of human love. In the final analysis, poets and novelists will have more to say about love than psychologists, for they express the inexpressible, and describe individual persons and their love problems, with their individual solutions and failures, and this is true to life and to eros.

I have been discussing the role of the feminine archetype in the psychology of men. It is now necessary to say some things about how the feminine archetype appears in the psychology of women in different ways and creates, as a result, different types of personalities.

In a paper entitled "Structural Forms of the Feminine

---

[19] Von Franz, *The Golden Ass*, p. XIII–1.

Psyche,"[20] the late Zurich analyst Toni Wolff described four
types of women: the mother, the hetaira, the amazon, and the
medium (medial). Toni Wolff argues that although every woman
embodies each of these four types in herself, one or more of them
tends to be of primary importance, and this primary identification gives to a woman's personality a particular form.

The woman who is most identified with *mother* finds her
primary identity and fulfillment in nourishing life. Usually she
will be fulfilled in bearing and raising children, and it is to this
that such a woman will primarily be drawn; when she marries,
the children will tend to be more important to her than her husband. She is of great value to people because she nourishes life,
although there is always the negative possibility that in her need
to be mother she may unconsciously retard the development of
her children, holding them to her for too long a time, or she may
marry a man who is psychologically crippled so that he too is a
child for her.

The word *hetaira* refers to a class of women in ancient
Greece who were especially educated so they could be psychological companions to men. The hetaira woman finds her primary
identity and fulfillment in achieving relationships with men.
These relationships may or may not include sexual love, but they
certainly will include psychological relating on all levels. Her instinct is to relate to a man and draw out his eros. Men often find
such a woman very valuable, for she is able to elicit a development in the area of personal interaction and love that otherwise
might be lost to them. There is always the danger, however, that
such a woman may be unable to achieve or remain in a lasting relationship, but may move continually from one man to another,
always making a relationship but not being capable of seeing it
through the vicissitudes of life. Needless to say, such a woman is
not likely to be as popular with other women as she is with men.

The *amazon* type is the woman who finds her primary identity and fulfillment in the outer world. In our society this will
usually be in some type of career. She does what men do, and of-

---

[20] Edward Whitmont also has a good summary in his book *The Symbolic
Quest*, pp. 178–181.

ten is capable, resourceful, and skillful at her work, making significant social contributions as a doctor, scientist, administrator, secretary, or whatever it might happen to be. Many greatly admired women have no doubt been of this type, all the way from Queen Elizabeth I to Susan B. Anthony. The dangerous possibility for such women is, however, that they may become too masculine in their orientation and lose contact with their feminine nature.

The *medium* or medial type is hardest to describe because we have practically no provision in our society for such a person. These women find their primary identity and fulfillment in making a relationship with the collective unconscious and being, as it were, a bridge between the world of the unconscious and the human community. These women may be visionaries, mystics, psychics, healers, poets, or mediums. Generally we look at them with all the suspicion that we direct toward the unconscious. In other cultures than our own, such women might have been priestesses or prophetesses, shamanesses or sybils. In our culture there is little place for them, and their often considerable psychological gifts being unfulfilled, they may experience difficulty adjusting to other more socially approved vocations in life and feel overwhelmed by the proximity of the unconscious. The medial type of woman may have a great contribution to make to the healing of mankind. Joan of Arc, for instance, no doubt had a great deal of the medial type in her, as did the so-called Witch of Endor who healed King Saul of his lack of courage and sent him out to die like a man and a hero.[21] On the negative side, unless her gifts are balanced by a certain scientific attitude or psychological insight, she may fall prey to inflation or to wildly speculative ideas.

It will be noted that the mother and hetaira are personally oriented, and people and relationships are of primary importance to them. The amazon and medial types are more impersonally oriented, the one being impersonally related to the outer world, the other to the world of the psyche.

It is also to be noted that a woman may fulfil one part of herself, and later be drawn to fulfil another. So a woman may

[21] 1 Sam. 28.

complete herself as mother, then find the hetaira or the amazon rising up in herself demanding fulfillment as well. Tension between one or more of these structural forms, which obviously may conflict with each other, may greatly complicate her psychological and social situation.

It is also to be noted that men who think of women only as mothers and wives will have difficulty understanding and accepting a woman who finds that she must fulfil herself as an amazon or medial type as well. A married man who attempts to suppress these other aspects of his wife can expect only trouble and unhappiness as a result. If he is able to accept his wife's other side, should it turn up, he may find himself ultimately blessed by the love of a more complete and fulfilled woman.

In these different types of women the animus may have a different weight, or at least come up with a different quality. He appears to be the strongest force in the amazon, who, as we noted, runs the danger of becoming *too* identified with her masculine side. He seems to play the least role in the hetaira, though he can be seen there too in the ruthlessness with which such a woman may pursue her love goals in relationship to a man.

The hetaira woman introduces an intriguing question: Does the quality of anima belong only to the man? Or are the terms *anima* and *animus* descriptive of feminine and masculine elements within both men and women?

As we have seen, the way in which Jung used these terms reserved anima as the name for the feminine qualities in a man, and animus as the name for the masculine qualities in a woman. He once wrote, "The anima, being of feminine gender, is exclusively a figure that compensates the masculine consciousness."[22] By the kind of parallel thinking that Jungians love, the same would be said of the animus: that he is exclusively a figure of feminine psychology, the personification of her masculine element that compensates her feminine consciousness. The idea is that a woman *is* feminine to begin with, and a man *is* masculine, so it is simply a matter of designating the contrasexual aspect that rules the unconscious.

However, James Hillman challenges this thesis in the *Spring*

---

[22] Jung, *CW* 7, par. 328.

articles referred to earlier. Exploring the argument that the anima cannot be limited to the male sex alone (and the corresponding argument could be used for the animus), Hillman notes that the anima is an archetype and "an archetype as such cannot be attributed to or located within the psyche of either sex."[23] He argues that the anima as archetype should be released from the notion of contrasexuality (that is, that it is the feminine opposite to masculine consciousness), for it can be seen to apply to the psychology of women as well. It would appear then that women, too, need to discover anima, the elemental feminine soul within themselves, and that the complaint of many women, that they feel inwardly empty, points to the area of soul as their need. It cannot be said that a woman has soul merely by virtue of her birth. She, too, must find the soul (anima) who is the wellspring of her inward life. And just as a man may develop his spirit and logos to the exclusion of his feminine side, and so lose his soul, so, too, a woman may develop the animus (the spirit) and exclude her soul in the process. Indeed, Hillman argues, many women today, in their pursuit of academic studies and masculine-oriented goals, suffer as a result from exactly the same problem as men: loss of anima or soul.

This is a particularly trying problem in the field of psychotherapy. Above all, the psychotherapist needs to have "soul" in order to be able to help his or her patients. Yet the process of training through which the prospective therapist must go, be that person a psychiatrist, psychologist, or some other type of counselor, is likely to produce a one-sided and collective person whose consciousness has been poured into a rationalistic straitjacket and who has, as a result, lost contact with anima or soul.

The instance of the so-called anima woman tends to substantiate Hillman's point. The anima woman is a woman who has a particular knack for gathering in, and reflecting back, a man's anima projection. She is said to catch, mirror, and mimic the anima in men, and so to fascinate and beguile them. It has been argued that instead of having an authentic personality of her own, such a woman lives out the anima of the man for him, while she herself is like an empty vessel. Hillman argues, however, that

---

[23] Hillman, "Anima," p. 111.

such women are not empty vessels at all, but that we are dealing here with a type of woman who lies very close to the elemental feminine quality called anima. She possesses and radiates anima as a quality of her own, and gathers in men's anima projections because she herself *is* anima. The apparent emptiness, he continues, "would be considered an authentic archetypal manifestation of the anima in one of her classical forms, maiden, nymph, Kore, which Jung so well describes (CW 9,1; para. 311) and where he also states that 'she often appears in woman.' "[24] What is lacking in such a woman would not be personality, for her personality is defined by the anima quality, especially in its maiden aspect, but rather by her failure to differentiate her individuality. Her danger is remaining too closely identified with an archetype, and failing to achieve her individual relatedness to her marked anima nature.

That Jung himself seemed to sense that anima was a quality belonging to women as well as to men is expressed in a letter he wrote in 1951 to Fr. Victor White about an unusual woman client. He comments,

I have seen Mrs. X and I assure you she is quite an eyeful and beyond! We had an interesting conversation and I must admit she is quite remarkable. *If ever there was an anima* it is she, and there is no doubt about it.

In such cases one had better cross oneself, because the anima, particularly when she is quintessential as in this case, casts a metaphysical shadow which is long like a hotel-bill and contains no end of items that add up in a marvellous way. One cannot label her and put her into a drawer. She decidedly leaves you guessing. I hadn't expected anything like that. At least I understand now why she dreams of Derby winners: it just belongs to her! She is a synchronistic phenomenon all over, and one can keep up with her as little as with one's own unconscious.

I think you ought to be very grateful to St. Dominicus that he has founded an order of which you are a member. In such cases one appreciates the existence of monasteries. It is just as well that she got all her psychology from books, as she would have busted

---

[24] Ibid., p. 118.

every decent and competent analyst. I sincerely hope that she is going on dreaming of winners, because such people need money to keep them afloat.[25]

We do not know who this remarkable woman is who made such an impression on Dr. Jung and Fr. White, but she evidently has an elusive, distinct feminine quality, a primitive soul, as it were, and in this case it is not a matter of this being projected onto her by a man; rather, it belongs to her as a woman. This would seem to give credence to Hillman's thesis that "anima" properly refers to an elemental feminine quality in men and women alike, and "animus," by the Jungian logic of opposites, likewise to an elemental masculine quality. This way of looking at things is reflected in the Chinese conception of psychic energy as flowing between two polarities. As mentioned earlier, the Chinese envisaged Yang and Yin as ubiquitous, cosmic, psychic poles of equal weight and value. The ancient Chinese document "T'ai I Chin Hua Tsung Chich," for example, spoke of the p'o soul and hun soul, feminine and masculine respectively, and said they were both in each individual.

An interesting passage in Esther Harding's book *Woman's Mysteries* also points to the presence in women, as well as in men, of an elemental feminine quality best called anima. Harding first describes the anima in man as a "feminine nature-spirit, which reflects the characteristics of the daemonic, nonhuman moon goddess, and gives to man a direct experience of the nonhuman Eros in all its power, both glorious and terrible." She then continues:

> With the woman the situation is somewhat different. She usually does not experience the feminine principle directly in this daemonic form. For it is mediated to her through her own womanhood and her own developed feeling approach to life. But if she will stop long enough to look within, she also may become aware of impulses and thoughts which are not in accord with her conscious attitudes but are the direct outcome of the crude and un-

---

[25] Jung, *Letters* 2, p. 24. Italics mine.

tamed feminine being within her. For the most part, however, a woman will not look at these dark secrets of her own nature. It is too painful, too undermining of the conscious character which she has built up for herself; she prefers to think that she really is as she appears to be. And indeed it is her task to stand between the Eros which is within her, and the world without, and through her own womanly adaptation to the world to make human, as it were, the daemoniac power of the nonhuman feminine principle.[26]

This "nonhuman feminine principle," according to Harding, is an elemental feminine spirit a woman may discover in herself, just as a man discovers it in himself, and it is just this that Hillman suggests is anima.

This also brings up the question of whether the anima is a unipersonality or a multipersonality. Jung's original thought was that the anima had a unified personality, but that the animus represented himself as a number of men and was a multipersonality. It is hard, however, to see what empirical basis there is for this idea. In a man's dreams there may appear any number of different women, just as in the dreams of a woman there may appear any number of different men. It is prejudicial to say in the former case that this is not as it "should" be, and that the various women figures in a man's dream mean a breaking up of a unipersonality. For it could just as easily be said that the dream in which many women appear represents the many feminine elements in that man's soul, or, at least, the many different faces of the feminine archetype. It is true, of course, that in the dreams of women many men sometimes appear. A woman may dream, for example, of a court of male figures, or a number of men sitting around a table, or a group of soldiers. Jungian psychologists then feel comfortable and say, "Ah! There is the animus as a number of men just as he should be! All these men personify the different opinions of the animus!" However, a woman may just as readily dream of a single man who appears as robber, lover, guide, priest, or whatever it may be. If in the earlier examples it was the ani-

---

[26] Esther Harding, *Woman's Mysteries, Ancient and Modern*, (New York: G. P. Putnam's Sons, 1971 edition), pp. 35, 36.

mus as the "many opinions," then what is it in the other cases
when the animus appears as a single person?

Indeed, we cannot even say for sure whether the "negative
anima" and "positive anima," the "negative animus" and "positive animus" (to use these stilted terms), are separate realities or
two sides of one coin. It is usually said that they represent the
dark and light sides of one reality, the destructive and helpful
sides of a single archetype. Yet, experientially, they appear as
quite distinct from each other, and certainly in practical life and
analysis we do well to differentiate between them and speak of
them as though they were separate beings.

That the anima, as well as the animus, can appear as multi-
ple figures is seen, of course, in mythology. In Greek mythology,
for instance, there are innumerable goddesses. Athena, Aphrodite, Demeter, Hera, and Artemis make up the five major goddesses of the upper world, and there are also Kore and Hecate of
the underworld, not to mention lesser goddesses such as Hestia
and innumerable nymphs and nixies. In his helpful article "Goddesses in Our Midst,"[27] Philip Zabriskie discusses the five goddesses of the upper world, whom he regards as a kind of "typolo-
gy of the feminine." Each goddess, he suggests, is different, and
each is "an image of a genuine, ancient, valid mode of the feminine." Aphrodite personifies "that aspect of the feminine which
continually seeks union with the masculine, for the erotic magnetism which powerfully pulls opposites to unite." Hera is the feminine that is also related to the male world but "impersonally,"
even "institutionally," rather than intensely and individually, for
as Queen of Olympus she guards the sanctified institutions of
throne and home. Demeter is related to the child, not to the
male, and embodies the elemental feminine power to "give birth,
to love, to nourish." Artemis, goddess of the amazons, virgin,
chaste, sufficient unto herself, is the feminine in an impersonal
aspect, and can be seen as dominant in "women of grace, vitality,
freedom, un-stuckness, perhaps even psychic powers," Athena,
also a virgin goddess, hence complete-in-herself, born from the

---

[27] Philip Zabriskie, "Goddesses in Our Midst," *Quadrant*, no. 17, Fall
1974.

head of her father, Zeus, personified the feminine as concerned with "the world of consciousness, of time, of ego, of work and growth."

In these five goddesses Zabriskie sees the models of certain typically feminine modes of life and behavior. They are all, to be sure, aspects of the one Great Goddess, but nevertheless appear as distinct personifications. The goddesses are still alive in the psychology of women, and, depending on which goddess is dominant in the psychology of a woman, give to her personality a distinct stamp. The hetaira, for instance, would have Aphrodite uppermost in her psyche; the mother, Demeter; the amazon, Athena perhaps, and the medium, Artemis, while Hera would be seen in those women who devote themselves to the causes of home, community, church, and so forth. But the goddesses do not appear only in women, they appear also in men, and personify the typical aspect of that man's soul. A Dr. Zhivago would certainly be moved by the spirit of Aphrodite, and the chaste, free-running long-distance runner, content in his solitude, by Artemis.

Zabriskie's article adds credence to the thought that the anima is no more a unipersonality than the animus, and that she can, in fact, be best represented by many different faces. He also confirms Hillman's thought that anima and animus are terms applicable to men and women alike.

These issues cannot be decided here and now, and that is as it should be, for anima and animus remain somewhat borderline concepts, verifiable in experience, useful in therapy, practical when we apply them to ourselves, but at the same time not capable of being precisely defined. When we shine the flashlight of our understanding on them we see them at first fairly clearly, but the farther back our eye travels along the beam of our light, the less distinct they appear to be. For practical purposes, it is perhaps better to stick with Jung's original definition and reserve the anima as a term for masculine psychology, and the animus for feminine psychology, but it would be a mistake to cast this into the form of a dogma and *insist* that this be so. For in dealing with the anima and the animus we are dealing with figures that are largely unconscious to us. Try as we might, the light of conscious discrimination does not penetrate deeply enough into the dimly lit and labyrinthine passages of the unconscious to perimit us to make any final statements.

The most important contribution Jung makes in his concepts of the anima and animus is to give us an idea of the polarity that exists within each of us. We are not homogenous units of psychic life, but contain an inevitable opposition within the totality that makes up our being. There are opposites within us, call them what we like—masculine and feminine, anima and animus, Yin and Yang—and these are eternally in tension and are eternally seeking to unite. The human soul is a great arena in which the Active and the Receptive, the Light and the Dark, the Yang and the Yin, seek to come together and forge within us an indescribable unity of personality. To achieve this union of the opposites within ourselves may very well be the task of life, requiring the utmost in perseverance and assiduous awareness. Usually men need women for this to come about, and women need men. And yet, ultimately the union of the opposites does not occur *between* a man who plays out the masculine and a woman who plays out the feminine, but *within* the being of each man and each woman in whom the opposites are finally conjoined.

It will be clear by now that the erotic imagery that comes when the anima and animus begin to emerge into consciousness has behind it the urge toward wholeness. The desire of the soul to unite with consciousness and forge an indivisible and creative personality is the most powerful urge within us. On this level, the urge toward wholeness and the urge to find God are identical, and so this urge to wholeness or individuation is also called by Jung the religious instinct. The image of the *Coniunctio*, of the union of the opposites, of the joining together of the male and female, is the image par excellence of the joining together of the conscious and unconscious parts of the personality. That is why so many of our dreams, and the parables of Jesus as well, concern weddings—apt symbols of the union of the opposites toward which the living energy within us strives.

In the final analysis, the opposites can be united only within an individual personality. The union of male and female cannot be achieved while we unconsciously project one half onto a human partner and act out the other half. Rather, as Nicholas Berdyaev noted, "it is only the union of these two principles (masculine and feminine) that constitutes a complete human being."[28] We are not the prince or princess who is going to unite with that person who is going to play out for us the role of our mystical partner. Rather, the prince and the princess, the divine pair, unite within us in a great nuptial action in the unconscious.

For this reason, if our human relationships are to succeed we must be able to distinguish between the divine and the human partners in our lives. This is why psychology speaks so often of the need to "withdraw projections." As we have seen, we can never completely withdraw all projections. The psychic images of the anima and animus are so rich and so unknown to us that they will always be projected. But it does mean that we learn to recognize when a projection has occurred. This act of consciousness gives us the possibility of integrating projected unconscious contents bit by bit, and, equally important, of making the vital distinction in our own minds between what is a projected archetypal image on the one hand and a human being on the other. For the divine partners in our lives are the anima and the animus, and their love affairs are matters for the gods. The human partners are the actual men and women in our lives, and while their love may *seem* at first to be ordinary and mundane when compared to the fire and mystery of divine love, yet both human and divine love can be fulfilled only when we are able to distinguish between them.

A final word may be in order about the relationship of our discourse to a religious understanding of marriage and sexuality. A proper Christian understanding of marriage, for instance, is based on the archetypal image of the *Coniunctio*. The church regards the marriage relationship as a representation on the human level of the divine mystery of the union of Christ with the soul, which has been the church's particular formulation of the archetype of the union of the opposites. By holding up to people the distinction between the union of Christ with the soul on the one

---

[28] Berdyaev, *Destiny of Man*, p. 62.

hand, and the human marriage relationship on the other, the
church has maintained an important distinction between the divine and the human dimensions of love.

Christian mysticism has long been fascinated with the image
of the *Coniunctio,* and justly so, since it symbolizes so profoundly
the relationship with God that the Christian was seeking. So
Christ was likened by the Church Fathers to a bridegroom, the
soul was his bride, and the cross was the marriage bed on which
the union of Christ with the soul was consummated. Saint Augustine wrote:

> Like a bridegroom Christ went forth from his chamber, he went
> out with a presage of his nuptials into the field of the world.
> . . . He came to the marriage-bed of the cross, and there, in mount-
> ing it, he consummated his marriage. And when he perceived the
> sighs of the creature, he lovingly gave himself up to the torment in
> place of his bride, and he joined himself to the woman for ever.[29]

Some Gnostics told the legendary story of Christ going to a
mountain, producing a woman from his side, and having intercourse with her. To a chaste Christian ear this story may sound
offensive, but, as Jung has pointed out, the Gnostics did not intend it that way. They were simply "stammering" in their efforts
to express the elusive but numinous image of totality as a union
of Christ with the soul.[30]

Because of its rich imagery, Christian mystics particularly
loved the *Song of Songs,* that most erotic book of the Bible. For
the mystic this erotic imagery was not simply sensuality, but was
the vehicle for conveying the image of the union of God with the
soul. As Evelyn Underhill wrote, ". . . the mystic loved the Song
of Songs because he there saw reflected, as in a mirror, the most
secret experiences of his soul."[31] Origen may have been the first
to elaborate on these erotic images of wholeness,[32] though the

[29] Quoted in C. G. Jung's *Symbols of Transformation, CW* 5, (Princeton,
N.J.: Princeton University Press, 1974), p. 269 n. 152.

[30] Jung, *Aion,* CW 9, 2, pp. 202–203.

[31] Evelyn Underhill, *Mysticism* (New York: E. P. Dutton and Company,
Inc., 1930 edition), p. 137.

[32] Cf. Hom. in Cant. 1.7.

list of Christian mystics who used this book as a source for reflections on the relationship of God to man is a long one, including Bishop Methodius, who went so far as to declare that as Christ unites with the soul each person becomes himself or herself a Christ.[33]

The use of the *Song of Songs* as a mystical document did not end with the apostolic era, but continued through Christian history until modern times. For instance, in the twelfth century Saint Bernard of Clairvaux elaborated on the image of the *Coniunctio* of Christ with the soul in a series of moving sermons based on the *Song of Songs*, and regarded the sensuous imagery of the book as a fitting conveyor for the divine mystery of the relationship of God with mankind, which was better reflected as a great love affair than as anything else.

So the language of the *Coniunctio* is part of the treasure of the church. However, the church today may need the language and knowledge of psychology in order to convey its treasure to the modern mind. The difficulty is that the church has, in recent centuries, lost its original connection with the human psyche. The teachings of Jesus are, as I have shown elsewhere,[34] filled with psychological meaning, and many of the early Christian Fathers were psychologists who wrote treatises on the soul and on dreams. The current denial on the part of the church of the reality of the psyche is unfortunate, for the union of Christ with the soul cannot be accomplished if the soul herself is denied and repressed. Since the Invisible Partners are the doorways through which we must pass to enter into the inner life, this means that they too need recognition as living realities.

Perhaps one reason for the refusal of the church to acknowledge the reality of man's soul lies in its fear of sexuality. Unlike Saint Bernard, who was not afraid to contemplate the sensuous imagery of the *Song of Songs*, the church as a whole has been

---

[33] Methodius, "The Banquet of the Ten Virgins," Ch. VIII, Ante-Nicene Fathers (Eerdmans Press, Vol. VI), p. 337. See also St. Augustine, "Concerning the Faith of Things Not Seen," par. 10; and Cyprian, "Treatises," *Ante-Nicene Fathers*, Vol. V, p. 523.

[34] John A. Sanford, *The Kingdom Within*, (New York: J. B. Lippincott Co., 1970).

frightened by man's sexual instinct and has sought to repress or
deny it. At times this fear of sexuality has become a mania. Saint
Augustine, for instance, called woman the devil's gateway, and
tried to envision some other way the human race might have
been reproduced without the benefit of woman. Sexual intercourse, he stated, was allowable only for the purpose of propagation; if even married persons enjoyed the act it was a sin. Saint Jerome urged husbands to honor their wives by abstaining from
intercourse with them, and claimed that to engage in sexual intercourse with one's wife was an insult to her. (As far as we know
he did not consult the wives regarding their feelings in the matter.) He went so far as to deny the sacrament to married persons
for several days after they had performed intercourse, on the basis that the purity of the sacrament would be defiled by the sexual act. Peter Lombard once warned Christians that the Holy
Spirit left the room when a married couple had sexual relationships, even if it was for the purpose of conceiving a child. If sexual life within marriage bordered on sin, one can imagine the evil
that fell on one if sexuality were experienced outside of marriage!
There was, to be sure, the sanctity of the Virgin Mary in Christian thought, and one can be grateful that the feminine image was
not entirely excluded from Christian imagery, but even she has
emerged in Christian imagery as a stainless woman who con-
ceived without benefit of a man, whose own birth was immacu-
late, and who remained a virgin throughout her life. Thus the
church has expressed its fear of woman, earth, and sensuality.

Such a fear is not shared by Judaism, however, which from
the beginning saw the act of intercourse between man and woman as a holy act. Certain Jewish groups even today prescribe for
scholars and rabbis that the Sabbath worship shall be ushered in
on Friday evening with sexual union between a man and his wife.

In taking her stand, the church has separated, in Gnostic
fashion, heaven and earth, spirit and matter, soul and body, and
in so doing has damaged the human spirit, and has been false to
its own message of the Incarnation. The original intent of the
church was, perhaps, to preserve mankind's hard-won spiritual-
ity from becoming lost in a sea of sensuality. The spirit and flesh,
the spirit and matter, are not so easily reconciled, and the one is

readily inundated by the other. No doubt the church felt it must throw in its lot with man's spiritual development, his sensuality already being sufficiently strong. The result, however, has not been the unification of personality, but the denial of wholeness, and a swing from one opposite to the other. So in Western history we have a continual seesawing back and forth of extremes of spiritual ascetisim on the one hand, and sensuality on the other. Nor have the values of the spirit ever been realized through the repression of the senses, for often the spirit is reached through the senses, and sometimes spiritual development arouses and needs sensual love in order to be grounded and become substantial. In seeking to avoid the conflict of the opposites by the denial of one side of life, damage has been done to the spirit of wholeness.

And yet it is strange that Christianity should for so long have tolerated a teaching about sexuality that declared that its sole justification was the propagation of the species. As Nicholas Berdyaev has pointed out, this "is transferring the principle of cattle-breeding to human relations,"[35] and is a denial of Christianity's highest value: human personality. For, as Berdyaev notes, sexual love can be entered into in order to express love, personality, and relationship, as well as for the purpose of propagating children. A Christian understanding of sexuality as an expression of the hungering of man for the fulfillment of relationship and personality would seem far more consistent with a religion that has stressed the incarnation of God in an earthly human life.

What is needed is not a denial of sexuality and eros, but the purification of eros from egocentricity, possessiveness, and unconsciousness. Eros is not identical with sexuality, but when sexuality is repressed eros is repressed too. Eros is a mighty power, which is at the heart of all human creativity, all love between people, even at the heart of the relationship between a human being and God. Eros warms all life, gives hope to living beings, and alone makes a sacrificial life possible. But when a human being wishes to claim eros as his or her own, to lay hold on the mystery

---

[35] Berdyaev, *Destiny of Man*, p. 240.

of the *Coniunctio* as his or her private possession, then eros is corrupted by greed and possessiveness, and its promise of higher consciousness is negated.

For these reasons, a Christian theology of marriage should call not for the denial of eros and sexuality, but for a heightened awareness of eros and what it means. The great Christian virtue of agape is not reached by denying eros, but by the purification of eros. Just as gold must be extracted from the ore by sifting and purifying the ore, so must the gold of human eros be purified by the sifting out of the impurities of human egocentricity. But no one ever obtained the gold by throwing out the ore. For this to be accomplished in our day, psychological awareness, as well as spiritual sensitivity, is needed. The mighty power of eros can become destructive if it is blind, and eros *is* blind as long as the human beings who carry in themselves this mighty power are blind and do not understand their own natures. Eros needs the enlightenment of a developed consciousness in order to reach its proper goal. Yet, without eros, consciousness cannot develop and the goal cannot be reached.

In the last analysis, eros is a great mystery. We can talk of sexuality, we can understand projections, we can speak of the transference, but when we add it all up it comes to zero, for it ends at the great mystery of Love.

Appendix: Active Imagination*

Psychological analysis alone is not enough to bring about the healing of the soul. Even though we understand all of our personal past history, and see the forces at work in us that have shaped our lives, this by itself will not heal us. The chief value of such analysis is that it gives us conscious orientation and a certain perspective. It also generally increases ego strength, thus freeing us to make certain choices and find new attitudes. All of this is very helpful, but not enough. Something more must˙be done in order to reconcile the conscious and the unconscious, to alter a destructive inner situation, or bring new life. This calls for some means of establishing and keeping alive the ongoing relationship with the inner world out of which new life comes and through which eventually our conflicts may be resolved.

One special tool for working with the unconscious that was developed by C. G. Jung is "active imagination." Active imagination goes a step beyond meditation. Meditation involves the contemplation of an image; active imaginaton is interaction with an image. The technique of active imagination brings into focus an image, voice, or figure of the unconscious and then enters into an interaction with that image or figure. In active imagination the ego is definitely a participant. We are not passively watching, but are positively involved in what is happening. It calls for an activation of the image from the unconscious *and* an alert and participating ego.

* Originally published in Chapter 6 of my book *Healing and Wholeness*, Paulist Press, 1977.

One word of caution: Active imagination can start a flow of images from the unconscious that, in a few cases, may be difficult to stop. This can be frightening, for the images are then like a flow of water that cannot be turned off and there is the fear of being inundated from within. I have never known anyone actually to be injured in this way, but I have known one or two people who became quite frightened. This is not likely to happen, for most people can turn off active imagination any time they want to, but it is a possibility if someone is too close to the unconscious and has not sufficient ego strength. In this case active imagination should not be undertaken without the guidance of a skilled spiritual director or therapist with whom the experiences can be shared if necessary.

Active imagination can begin in several ways. A dream is one place to start. In this case we continue the dream in our imagination as a story, writing down whatever comes to us. This is especially helpful in certain dreams that do not reach a conclusion. For instance, maybe we dream we are being pursued by some figure; we run and run and the dream suddenly ends while we are still running from this figure. This is an "unfinished" dream. It does not end because the unconscious cannot take the action any further. We can continue the dream by finishing its story in active imagination. What happens now as that figure pursues us? Perhaps we see ourselves stopping and facing our adversary, or maybe someone comes into the situation to help us. Any number of possibilities present themselves, but only one can be selected and this is the one we will follow through to see where it leads us.

A fantasy can also be utilized as the basis for active imagination. The place to begin would be with the fantasy that has been haunting our minds, the uninvited train of thought that keeps coming back to us again and again. Maybe it is a recurring fantasy of a burglar breaking into our house, or perhaps of some kind of doom descending on us, or perhaps it is a powerful sexual fantasy. One can take the fantasy and deliberately develop it, writing down whatever occurs to us as we continue the fantasy as a story. This has the effect of altering our psychological situation, and of making clearer the underlying meaning of the fantasy. With sexual fantasies this may be the only way to avoid living them out concretely in ways that may be destructive to our relationships.

One source for Jung's ideas on active imagination was alchemy. Alchemy spoke of the adept (alchemist) giving careful attention to all the elements in his retort and observing their transformation with great concentration. Jung transliterates the language of alchemy into its psychological equivalent and sees this as a prototype of active imagination. What alchemy suggests, he says, is that we

> take the unconscious in one of its handiest forms, say a spontaneous fantasy, a dream, an irrational mood, an affect, or something of the kind, and operate with it. Give it your special attention, concentrate on it, and observe its alterations objectively. Spare no effort to devote yourself to this task, follow the subsequent transformations of the spontaneous fantasy attentively and carefully. Above all, don't let anything from outside, that does not belong, get into it, for the fantasy-image has "everything it needs." In this way one is certain of not interfering by conscious caprice and of giving the unconscious a free hand.[1]

In the same volume, Jung puts it even more explicitly:

> This process can, as I have said, take place spontaneously or be artificially induced. In the latter case you choose a dream, or some other fantasy-image, and concentrate on it by simply catching hold of it and looking at it. You can also use a bad mood as a starting point, and then try to find out what sort of fantasy-image it will produce, or what image expresses this mood. You then fix this image in the mind by concentrating your attention. Usually it will alter, as the mere fact of contemplating it animates it. The alterations must be carefully noted down all the time, for they reflect the psychic processes in the unconscious background, which appear in the form of images consisting of conscious memory material. In this way conscious and unconscious are united, just as a waterfall connects above and below.[2]

---

[1] C. G. Jung, *Mysterium Coniunctionis,* *CW* 14 (Princeton, N.J.: Princeton University Press, 1963, 1974), p. 526.

[2] Ibid., p. 495.

Active imagination can be started from any manifestation of the unconscious—dream, affect, mood, or whatever—but the simplest place to start is with the daily running dialogue that goes on within the minds of most of us. We spend a lot of time "arguing" with ourselves. A little introspection will reveal that there are all kinds of voices battling inside of us. Often these inner dialogues resemble courtroom scenes, and it is as if we were on trial for something. There is the inner prosecutor, the critical voice that tries to convict us of this or that, and that also, as a rule, constitutes itself as judge as well as accuser. In a woman this voice usually has a masculine character, and in a man a feminine character. These "voices" are like autonomous thoughts or moods that suddenly inject themselves into our consciousness. If we are totally unaware of them, we become identical with them. If the voice we are hearing is the accusing voice of the inner critic or "prosecuting attorney," we become depressed, and our self-image goes down to zero. To become aware of the autonomous nature of these voices is to begin to make a distinction between them and us, and this dawning awareness brings the possibility of breaking free from what amounts to a state of being possessed.

To begin an active imagination with the argument we are hearing inside of us we start by writing down the thoughts already racing through our minds. It helps to personify the different voices we hear. The "Prosecuting Attorney," the "Great Score Keeper," the "Cynical Bystander," the "Forlorn Woman," are personifications of inner voices that certain people have used from time to time. The personification should, of course, correspond to the kind of voice we are hearing. Transferring the inner argument to paper makes it possible for us to respond to these autonomous thoughts, and encourages us to clarify and adopt our own point of view. By writing things down we really begin to hear what is being said, and are now in a position to examine these utterances for what they are. In doing this we may discover that the authority of the inner critic, for instance, may not be so great after all, that while this critic poses as God it is actually a personification of collective opinions, that is, of general or conventional points of view.

Writing things down also strengthens the ego, for to take pen in hand and begin to write is an ego activity, and has the effect of solidifying and centering consciousness, and affirming it in the face of destructive influences. Hence it now becomes possible to find our position and, perhaps, turn the tables on an inner enemy who, up until now, has had the advantage of being able to work in the dark.

Of course it can also be a positive voice that we hear and with which we learn to talk. Just as there is a negative voice that seems to want us to fail in life, so there is a positive voice that gives us helpful insights and flashes of inspiration. We can cultivate a relationship with this side of ourselves by learning to dialogue with it, and talk over with it our life situation.

The ancients used to call such a figure a *spiritus familiaris*. Socrates referred to it as his "daimon," meaning not "demon" in the negative sense of the word, but his "genius" or inspirational spirit. In Christian parlance it is a version of the guardian angel or a manifestation of the guidance of the Holy Spirit. Psychologically this positive figure can be likened to a personification of the Self as it relates to ego consciousness. If a relationship with this inner figure can be developed, we are greatly helped. It is like having an inner analyst or spiritual director. In some cases it is the way to freedom from dependence on an analyst, for it gives us access to our own unconscious wisdom.

Notice how many times I have said that in doing active imagination we must write it down. There are many reasons for putting active imagination in writing. Writing gives reality to it; unless it is written it may seem wispy and vaporish and lack impact. Writing things down also keeps us from cheating on the process. It may be that there are some unpleasant things we have to learn about ourselves and it is easy to avoid these unless they are written. Writing also, as mentioned, strengthens the hand of the ego and develops our conscious position in the face of the unconscious. Finally, it gives us a permanent record and enables us from time to time to review what we have done. Not only does this refresh the memory, but there are times when something has emerged in active imagination that we could not understand at the time but is clear to us later.

There is one exception to the practice of recording active imagination; sometimes it works best when we are in a meditative state, and writing it down might interrupt. Pursue the active imagination while meditating, but then record it immediately in a journal.

I mentioned the risk in doing active imagination, but the greater difficulty lies in getting people to do it at all. Some of this has to do with the fact that it must be written to become real. To write down active imagination is work. In fact, active imagination itself is hard work; it takes discipline, and to do it we must overcome the inertia that grips us when it comes to psychological matters. People are lazy about their own psyches. We do not want to have to work on ourselves, but want everything to come to us. This is a common difficulty the therapist encounters: He finds that people come to him expecting him to have some magic with which to make everything all right, and they won't have to do the work themselves. Not only is this exhausting for the therapist, who has to provide more than his share of energy for the process, but the client does not make satisfactory progress, for the fact is that we get well in direct proportion to the energy we put into our psychological development.

In addition to the lazy streak in us, which resists doing active imagination precisely because it is "active," there is also the voice within us that is certain to comment that it is "nothing but your own thoughts." As soon as we depart from the known and conventional, this cynical, doubting voice begins to comment that what we are doing is nonsense, banal, or not worth writing down. It is another aspect of the critical voice we have met before, and may also say to us when we awaken with a dream, "Oh, that dream doesn't mean anything." People who try to do creative writing are certain to run into this voice too, and will hear it say things such as, "Oh, that has already been written," or, "You will never be able to get it published." This voice will try to keep us from doing active imagination, and will make poisonous comments as though it wants to keep our development on the most mediocre level possible. It acts like a negative-mother-voice in a man, or a poisonous-father voice in a woman, a version of the witch who, in fairy tales, paralyzes the young hero or heroine, turning them into stone, or sending them into sleep, or causing them to lose their heads.

There are two ways to deal with this voice as it relates to active imagination. One method is to resolutely go ahead anyway, to say something like, "I don't care what that voice says, I am going to do this active imagintion and when it is done we will see what it is like." The other method is to begin the active imagination by dialoguing with the voice itself. If we have it out with this voice to begin with we may find that the battle is half won and we are beginning to free ourselves from something paralyzing that has affected us on many levels of life.

In the dialogue form of active imagination it often works best to write down the first thoughts that come into our minds. We identify the voice with whom we wish to speak and say what we want, and then record the first "answering thought" that occurs to us. Then we answer back, and so the dialogue proceeds. It is important not to criticize or examine what is being said as we go along, but to proceed as if it were a normal conversation. Later, when it is all finished, we can go back over what we have written and examine it for some of its content if we wish.

Active imagination sometimes has more vitality than at other times. There are times when an image, voice, or fantasy is right there and becomes activated at once and interacts with us. At other times the results may not be so vital. Some people, for instance, may be able to do active imagination in the morning, but not in the evening. For others it may be the other way around. Each person must find his own way of working and discover what suits his personality the best.

Active imagination can be very long or very short. A good example of a long active imagination is found in Gerhard Adler's book *The Living Symbol*,[3] in which he discusses a series of active imaginations a woman did over many months, out of which there evolved a long and elaborate fantasy. On the other hand, active imagination may also be quite brief. The shortest active imagination I know of came to a writer who was attempting for the third time to revise a manuscript to please his publisher. Previously he had been able to make certain changes, but this time when he sat at his typewriter absolutely nothing came. For three days he was in depression as not a single thought or word came to him, although usually words flowed like water. At least it became clear

---

[3] Gerhard Adler, *The Living Symbol*, (New York: Pantheon Books, 1961).

that something in him was resisting revising the manuscript, so he decided to personify this resistance and talk to it. The resulting active imagination went like this;

Author (to his resistance): "Okay, why are you resisting doing this work?"

Answering voice (immediately): "Because it is already written."

That was it; there was nothing more that needed to be said. With this the author realized that the book was in its proper and completed form as it now stood, and if the publisher with whom he was corresponding did not want it that way he had to find another publisher. And this is exactly what happened.

Ultimately active imagination is helpful because it tends to reconcile the conscious and the unconscious. It takes us into a relationship with the figures of the unconscious, "negotiating" and working things out with them. This helps bring about that paradoxical union of the conscious and unconscious personalities that corresponds to what the alchemists called the *unio mentalis*. Just as the alchemists, in the search for the stone, started with materials that were commonly rejected, so we start with the otherwise rejected material of the unconscious and, through meditation or active imagination, activate an inner process. Jung, in a commentary on alchemical symbolism, gives us this apt description of how this process works to bring us closer to wholeness:

> Thus the modern man cannot even bring about the unio mentalis which would enable him to accomplish the second degree of conjunction. The analyst's guidance in helping him to understand the statements of his unconscious in dreams, etc. may provide the necessary insight, but when it comes to the question of real experience the analyst can no longer help him: he himself must put his hand to the work. He is then in the position of an alchemist's apprentice who is inducted into the teachings by the Master and learns all the tricks of the laboratory. But sometime he must set about the opus himself, for, as the alchemists emphasize, nobody else can do it for him. Like this apprentice, the modern man begins with an unseemly prima materia which presents itself in unexpected form—a contemptible fantasy which, like the stone that the builders rejected, is "flung into the street" and is so "cheap" that people do not even look at it. He will observe it from day to day and note its alter-

ations until his eyes are opened or, as the alchemists say, until the fish's eyes, or the sparks, shine in the dark solution. . . .

The light that gradually dawns on him consists in his understanding that his fantasy is a real psychic process which is happening to him personally. Although, to a certain extent, he looks on from outside, impartially, he is also an acting and suffering figure in the drama of the psyche. . . .If you recognize your own involvement you yourself must enter into the process with your personal reactions, just as if you were one of the fantasy figures, or rather, as if the drama being enacted before your eyes were real. It is a psychic fact that this fantasy is happening, and it is as real as you—as a psychic entity—are real. . . . If you place yourself in the drama as you really are, not only does it gain in actuality but you also create, by your criticism of the fantasy, an effective counterbalance to its tendency to get out of hand. For what is now happening is the decisive rapprochement with the unconscious. This is where insight, the *unio metalis*, begins to become real. What you are now creating is the beginning of individuation, whose immediate goal is the experience and production of the symbol of totality.[4]

While Jung is the one who first developed active imagination as a psychologically refined tool for working with the unconscious, it has been used before. A very good example of active imagination is found in Matthew's Gospel in the story of the Temptations in the Wilderness.[5] Jesus has gone into the wilderness to be alone after receiving the Holy Spirit from God and hearing the voice that proclaimed "This is my beloved Son, in whom I am well pleased." Naturally, the first thing that would happen after such an experience is an inflation, a temptation to take the experience in the wrong way, and this temptation is presented in the voice of Satan, who says, "If thou be the Son of God, command that these stones be made bread." Jesus hears that voice within himself and answers it. The voice then speaks a second time, and a third, and each time Jesus hears the voice and replies to it. This is active imagination. Nor is this a way of saying that the Satan in the story is not real. Such a voice within us is *very* real, so real that unless we hear it, recognize it for what it

---

[4] Jung, *Mysterium Coniunctionis,* pp. 528–529.
[5] Mt. 4:1–11 KJV.

is, and respond to it, we will likely be taken over by it. Had this happened to Jesus his whole life would have gone the wrong way. His dialogue with Satan was the cornerstone of the life and ministry that he built and is a vivid illustration of how vital active imagination can be.

Finally, note that the term is *active* imagination. It is not a technique in which the movements of the unconscious are simply observed. Rather the ego asserts itself in the process, and the demands of the unconscious must be measured against the reality of the ego. In his dialogue with Satan, Jesus' ego was very evident. He did not just hear the voice, but reacted to it and responded to it. Of course the dialogue might be with a helpful voice too, such as the dialogue Elijah had with Yahweh's voice in the cave on Mt. Sinai.[6] But in either event the process of active imagination calls for active participation by the ego, and represents an attempt of consciousness and the unconscious to have it out with each other and work out together a creative life.

[6] 1 Kings 19:9.

Bibliography

BOOKS

Bronte, Emily. *Wuthering Heights.* New York: Random House, Inc., 1943.

Castillejo, Irene de. *Knowing Woman.* New York: G. P. Putnam's Sons, 1973.
A highly provocative study of feminine psychology.

Drury, Michael, *To a Young Wife from an Old Mistress.* Garden City, New York: Doubleday and Company, Inc., 1966.
Wise, profound advice from one woman to another.

Franz, Marie-Louise von. *The Feminine in Fairy Tales.* Zurich: Spring Publications, 1972.
An excellent study of the feminine in men and women.

———. *Apuleius' The Golden Ass.* Zurich: Spring Publications, 1970, 1974.

———. *Individuation in Fairy Tales.* Zurich: Spring Publications, 1977.

Guggenbuhl-Craig, Adolf. *Marriage, Dead or Alive.* Zurich: Spring Publications, 1977.
Modern, timely thoughts on marriage, with good chapters on the meaning of sexuality.

Hannah, Barbara. *Striving Towards Wholeness.* New York: G. P. Putnam's Sons, 1971.
The chapters on the Brontë sisters and *Wuthering Heights* are an important contribution to feminine psychology and the psychology of the animus.

129

Harding, Esther. *The Way of All Women*. New York: David McKay Company, Inc., 1933, 1961.
An "old timer" now, but still valuable.

———. *Woman's Mysteries, Ancient and Modern*. New York: G. P. Putnam's Sons, 1971.
Valuable archetypal material on the nature of the feminine.

Johnson, Robert, *HE!* King of Prussia, Pa.: Religious Publishing Co., 1974.
A little jewel; a splendid study of the psychology of men.

———. *SHE!* King of Prussia, Pa.: Religious Publishing Co., 1976.
A succinct study of feminine psychology.

In the following Jung entries, consult the Table of Contents and the Index for passages regarding the anima and animus.

Jung, C. G. *Collected Works* [hereafter cited as *CW*] 7, *Two Essays in Analytical Psychology*. New York: Pantheon Books, 1953.

———. *CW* 9, 1, *The Archetypes of the Collective Unconscious*. New York: Pantheon Books, 1959.

———. *CW* 9, 2, *Aion*. New York: Pantheon Books, 1959.

———. *CW* 13, *Alchemical Studies*. Princeton, N. J.: Princeton University Press, 1967, 1970.

———. *CW* 14, *Mysterium Coniunctionis*. Princeton, N. J.: Princeton University Press, 1963, 1974.

———. *CW* 16, *The Practice of Psychotherapy*. New York: Pantheon Books, 1954.

———. *C. G. Jung Speaking*. Edited by William McGuire and R. F. C. Hull. Princeton, N. J.: Princeton University Press, 1977.

———. *Letters 1*. Princeton, N. J.: Princeton University Press, 1973.

———. *Letters 2*. Princeton, N. J.: Princeton University Press, 1975.

———. *Man and His Symbols*. Garden City, N. Y.: Doubleday and Company, Inc., 1964.

———. *Memories, Dreams, Reflections*. New York: Pantheon Books, 1963.

———. *Visions Seminars*, Part One and Part Two. Zurich: Spring Publications, 1976.

Jung, Emma. *Animus and Anima*. Zurich: Spring Publications, 1974.
Particularly good on the animus.

Neumann, Erich. *Amor and Psyche*. New York: Pantheon Books, 1956.
A study of the most significant myth of the feminine in Greek mythology.

Sanford, John A. *Healing and Wholeness*. New York: The Paulist Press, 1977.

The last chapter contains a summary of the process of active imagination, a useful tool in attempting to integrate the anima and animus.

————. *The Kingdom Within*. New York: J. B. Lippincott Co., 1970.
Chapters 9 and 10 contain material relevant to the anima and animus.

Singer, June. *Androgyny*. Garden City, N. Y.: Doubleday Company, Inc., 1976
A woman analyst looks at the problem of man/woman today with a special view to the problems facing modern women.

Ulanov, Ann B. *The Feminine in Jungian Psychology and in Christian Theology*. Evanston, Ill.: Northwestern University Press, 1971.

Whitmont, Edward C. *The Symbolic Quest*. New York: G. P. Putnam's Sons, 1969.
The closest thing there is to a textbook in Jungian psychology with good chapters on the masculine and feminine.

Wilhelm, Richard, trans. *The Secret of the Golden Flower*. New York: Harcourt, Brace & World, Inc., 1931; revised and augmented, 1962.

ARTICLES

Binswanger, Hilde. "Positive Aspects of the Animus." *Spring*, 1963.

Heisler, Verda. "Individuation in Marriage." *Psychological Perspectives* 1, no. 2, Fall 1970.
A valuable contribution to the psychology of marriage relationships.

Hillman, James. "Anima." *Spring*, 1973 and 1974.
Hillman boldly explores the concept of the anima and adds many new thoughts. Not for beginners, but thought-provoking.

Hough, Graham. "Poetry and the Anima." *Spring*, 1973.

Ostrowski, Margaret. "Anima Images in Carl Spitteler's Poetry." *Spring*. 1962.

Wolf, Toni, "Structural Forms of the Feminine Psyche."
This was privately printed and is out of print, but there is a good resume of it in Whitmont's book, already cited.

Zabriskie, Philip. "Goddesses in our Midst." *Quadrant*, no. 17, Fall 1974.
An important article on the nature of the feminine based on studies of five Greek goddesses.

PAMPHLETS

Hannah, Barbara. "The Problem of Contact with Animus." London: Guild of Pastoral Psychology, 1962.

————— "The Religious Function of the Animus in the Book of Tobit." London: Guild of Pastoral Psychology, 1961.

Heydt, Vera von der. "On the Animus." London: Guild of Pastoral Psychology, 1964.

Lander, Forsaith, "The Anima." London: Guild of Pastoral Psychology, 1962.

Metman, Eva, "Woman and the Anima." London: Guild of Pastoral Psychology, 1951.

Index

A

Actium, battle of, 23
active imagination, 42, 61n, 94, Appendix
agape, 118
Age of Faith, The, 21n
Aion, CW 9,2, 41n, 50n, 75n, 114n
alchemists, 3
Alchemical Studies, CW 13, 70n
American Indian(s), 3, 65, 93, 99
androgynous, 3, 4, 5, 6, 95, 98, 100
anger, 36, 37, 38, 39, 40, 50, 53
animare, 6
"Anima," 40n
anima: 12, 22, 25, 34, 35, 36, 37, 40, 41, 42, 43, 44, 49, 50, 53, 54, 55, 58, 60, 64, 66, 67, 68, 69, 70, 72, 75, 78, 84, 85, 86, 91, 100, 105, 106, 107, 108, 109; an archetype, 12, 66, 106; correct/proper place, 40, 65, 69–70; development, 68f; dialogue with, 61ff; double, 83, 87; and man's ego, 98; emotion(s), 37, 40, 41, 50–51; and eros, 67, 75; fantasies, 25, 59, 71, 72, 73, 82, 100; four stages, 68; hideous maiden/damsel, 57, 72; and homosexuality, 98, 99; how to defeat it, 43; image, 14, 21, 25, 72, 83, 84, 87; Jung's term/definition, 12, 42, 64, 111; match and gasoline 37, 49; mood(s) 35, 36, 43, 49, 59, 61, 71; mouthpiece/ bridge and the unconscious, 43, 64, 70, 72; neither good nor bad, 67; and persona, 70, 71; personification of, 64, 69, 70; positive/negative, 15, 32, 36, 38, 41, 42, 43, 60, 72, 110; possession, 35, 36, 41, 49, 51, 53, 54; power, 24, 32; projec- tion(s), 14, 15, 20, 24, 25, 67, 73, 83, 85, 106, 107; relation- ship, 35, 36, 40, 41, 67, 70, 71, 84; resentment, 36; and soul, 25, 66, 74, 106; uni/ multi-personality, 109, 111; as witch, 11, 15, 37, 43, 44, 49, 50, 51, 54; "_____ woman," 106
anima/animus: 1, 6, 7, 9, 10, 11, 12, 13, 17, 20, 31, 54, 58, 59,

133

Self, 94, 95; relationship, 13, 19, 20, 87; what we do with it, 20; withdrawal of, 59, 65, 83, 87, 113

psyche: 6, 14, 20, 61, 65, 77, 78, 83, 85, 87, 94, 104, 106, 111, 115; and projection, 11; growth and development, 66; man's, 12, 64; personified in mythology, 10; woman's, 47, 73

"Psychology of the Transference, The," 74

puer, 96

Puer Aeternus, 95n, 97n

R

rejection: 38, 53; by mother, 53

relationship(s): 1, 5, 14, 15, 16, 17, 18, 19, 20, 25, 28, 29, 33, 34, 37, 38, 39, 40, 41, 42, 52, 53, 54, 55, 58, 59, 60, 61, 62, 63, 67, 68, 70, 75, 79, 82, 84, 86, 87, 88, 91, 92, 93, 94, 104, 113, 117; anima/animus, 6, 30, 35, 36, 37, 40, 62, 63, 64, 67, 68, 69, 70, 71, 77, 84; being in love, 17, 18; between the sexes, 1, 13, 14, 15, 18, 19, 24, 25, 28, 34, 38, 39, 40, 49, 51, 54, 62, 63, 74, 80, 84, 96, 103; correct, 77, 79; container and contained, 27, 28; Dante and Beatrice, 21; diagram, 17, 29; Eros, 75; extramarital, 85; with God, 68, 114, 115, 117; heterosexual, 98; homosexual, 94, 96, 98, 99; to inner world, 66; love, 18–19, 20, 26, 48, 83, 105; marriage, 27, 80, 81, 82, 85, 114; and moods, 35, 36; to

persona, 70, 71; projection, 19, 87; to the psychic world, 10; with the Self, 96; sexual, 14, 19, 91, 96, 116; ultimate, 17, 19; and the unconscious, 33, 64, 83, 87; to the highest wisdom, 68; Yang and Yin, 8

resentment, 36

Romans, Epistle to the 7:19, 9n

S

St. Augustine, 114, 115n, 116
St. Bernard of Clairvaux, 115
St. Jerome, 116
St. Paul, 9
1 Samuel, Book of 18:10–11, 71n; ch. 28, 104n
Saul, King, 71, 104
Secret of the Golden Flower, The, 8, 9n, 61n, 64
self/Self: 76, 94, 95, 96; and ego, 96
senex, 96
Seven Arrows, 3n
sexuality, 4, 8, 68, 80, 89, 91, 92, 93, 94, 96, 100, 101, 102, 113, 115, 116, 117, 118
shadow: 9, 10, 14, 70; integration of, 10; metaphysical, 107
Shakespeare, 18
shaman(ess)(ism), 5, 99, 104
Shamanism, 5n
Sirens, 31f, 34
Song of Songs, 114, 115
soul(s): 2, 19, 20, 24, 34, 57, 58, 71, 73, 85, 106, 112, 114, 115, 116; androgynus, 95; anima, 6, 9, 66, 68, 70, 106; animus, 6, 9, 74ff; Babylonian mythology, 44; Dante's, 21, 24; feminine/masculine, 10, 67, 74, 75, 76, 77, 78, 106; hun,